Senior Citizens Writing

Senior Citizens Writing

A Workshop and Anthology,
with an Introduction and Guide
for Workshop Leaders

W. Ross Winterowd

Parlor Press
West Lafayette, Indiana
www.parlorpress.com

Parlor Press LLC, West Lafayette, Indiana 47906

© 2007 by Parlor Press
All rights reserved.
Printed in the United States of America
S A N: 2 5 4 - 8 8 7 9

Library of Congress Cataloging-in-Publication Data

Winterowd, W. Ross.
  Senior citizens writing : a workshop and anthology, with
an introduction and guide for workshop leaders / W. Ross
Winterowd.
    p. cm.
  ISBN 978-1-60235-000-7 (pbk. : alk. paper) -- ISBN 978-1-
60235-001-4 (adobe ebook)
  1. Autobiography. 2. Older people's writings, American. 3.
Aging--Literary collections. I. Title.
  CT25.W56 2007
  808'.06692--dc22
                                        2006035870

Printed on acid-free paper.
Cover and book design by David Blakesley
Cover images © 2006 by Dar Yang Yan. Used by permission.
Thanks to Megan Wellman for providing copy editing
  assistance on this project.

Parlor Press, LLC is an independent publisher of scholarly
and trade titles in print and multimedia formats. This book is
available in paperback and Adobe eBook formats from Parlor
Press on the Internet at http://www.parlorpress.com. For submission information or to find out about Parlor Press publications, write to Parlor Press, 816 Robinson St., West Lafayette,
Indiana, 47906, or e-mail editor@parlorpress.com.

Preface

Without the support of the Huntington Beach Union High School District administration and staff, the writing workshops that I have been conducting for the last five years would have been impossible. Dr. Doris Longmead, principle of the Coast High School and Adult School, has been unfailing in her support.

Three members of the school's staff have been invaluable allies, not only in providing logistical support, but also in supplying me with good cheer and wise guidance. I look forward to my weekly meetings with Lynne Bergman, an always reliable and ever-cheerful adjutant; June Stark-Karaba, whose stylishness is exceeded only by her sunny nature and efficiency; and Georgina "Gina" Amparan, who keeps me on schedule by plugging the gaps in my seventy-six-year-old memory and unfailingly supplying me with necessities, such as supplementary materials that I have prepared and that she reproduces.

My boss in the workshop endeavor is Catherine Mc-Gough, assistant principal at the school. For three decades, Cathy and I have been friends and colleagues, working with the school district first on "Project Literacy," a successful effort to improve students' skills in written language, and now with our ongoing work to give senior citizens an audience for their writing.

Ever with us, sometimes in person but always in spirit, is Norma Winterowd. After suffering a disastrous stroke in 1999, she went on to survive a series of health crises, and she still prevails, giving all who know her the bounty of her love.

—*W.R.W.*

Contents

Contents

Senior Citizens Writing

Introduction: Senior (Citizen) Composition

W. Ross Winterowd

Since 1997, I have been conducting writing workshops for senior citizens. During those years, I have learned a great deal more than have the participants in the workshops.

Statistics demonstrate that the proportion of seniors in our population is burgeoning and will continue to do so, with the result that colleges and universities have a new pool of prospective students who continue to grow intellectually and are eager to tell their stories, explain their philosophies, create fictions, and vent their anger at the injustices they perceive in the nation and the world. In other words, many seniors want to write. If they serve no other purposes, writing workshops give participants a stimulus for writing and an audience for their work.[1]

The Philosophy of Composition

As some readers of this volume know, I have during my career argued against what I have called the Romantic philosophy of composition, represented most notably by

Peter Elbow. This Romanticism emphasized expression over form; it advised students to look inward and find the stuff of discourse in their own beings; it stressed an undefined something called "voice" over style.

I believed, and I still believe, that the purpose of expository writing courses (i.e., "composition") in colleges and universities is to prepare students to enter the world of academic discourse, with the ability to explain processes and ideas clearly, to argue cogently and rationally, and to adapt to the forms demanded by the various disciplines. It was obvious to me that the Romantic philosophy of composition would shortchange students, and research validates my critique.[2]

However, much of the "Romantic" doctrine of composition applies necessarily, I think, to the writing of senior citizens in workshops. With their careers behind them, they want primarily to *express* themselves, not, certainly, in gushes of nostalgia or laments about the present, but in ways that they had no time, need, or motive for during their lives as engineers, lawyers, teachers, carpenters, plumbers, and mainstays of families. They write memoirs, of course—but also novels, philosophical musings, political arguments (and diatribes), explanations of technical and scientific processes and concepts, and humor. As my explanation of the workshops will make clear, there are no assignments, except "Write!"

Introduction

Instruction: A Community of Writers

The verb "teach" does not apply to the writing workshop, but the nouns "feedback" and "response" do characterize most of the "instruction" that takes place. The whole dynamic of the workshop is a community of writers responding to the writing of their colleagues. Hereafter, I will explain the mechanics of this process. The important concept is this: readers (*sans* PhDs in English!) can rapidly become skilled responders to texts, providing the rich feedback that enables writers to revise a text and to gain skills that transcend this or that given text. In other words, the workshop writers as readers "teach" one another the abilities needed for success. The workshop leader is a facilitator and responder, almost never a teacher in the traditional sense.

The "pedagogical method" of the workshops is simply to provide rich feedback on writers' texts. I encourage participants to make notes on the texts as they read them so that discussion can be focused. Frequently, but not always, a reader-participant will give his or her annotated copy of the text to its author. I take part in the discussions during each session, but I also distribute a handout that contains what I hope are constructive remarks on each piece of writing that has been submitted. (See Appendix for an example of my handouts.)

Voice: Style/Mechanics

In the academy, in businesses, and in the professions, writing "mechanics" count for a great deal. Orthography is next to godliness. Faulty agreement of pronouns with antecedents and verbs with subjects is a mortal sin. In the writing workshops, however, we play the game without the net of mechanical correctness. More accurately, we contextualize mechanical correctness. Within our circle, it makes no difference whether the tuber is spelled *potato* or *potatoe*, whether it's *differance* or *difference*. None of us gasp or sigh when we read "one of the problems were. . . ."

Exaggerated concern with mechanical correctness can bring the free flow of writing to a drip-drip-drip.

When a writer decides to submit a text to an audience outside our group, mechanical correctness does sometimes count, and the writer needs to clean the text up, perhaps with the help of someone who can spot and eliminate the gaffes.

Style in terms of sentence structure is quite another matter. Readers can ignore mechanical lapses, but they must mentally process the writer's sentences. Syntax is, to be sure, a matter of the esthetics of writing, but more than that, it can make texts either difficult or easy for readers to process. (In other words, style is in large part a concern of psycholinguistics.)

I can demonstrate this principle with the following two sentences:

1. That Bill thought that Jim believed that Mary is crazy is strange.
2. It is strange that Bill thought that Jim believed that Mary is crazy.

In brief, the first sentence is difficult to process because *strange*, the pivotal word or true predicate of the sentence is at the end, and the reader cannot achieve closure on the structure of the sentence until he or she arrives at that predicate. In the second sentence, the true predicate is up front, allowing the reader to process the rest of the sentence sequentially.

"Choppy" prose is also an esthetic and psycholinguistic problem.

1. The village of Holcomb stands on the high wheat plains of western Kansas. It is a lonesome area. Other Kansans call it "out there." It is some seventy miles east of the Colorado border. It has hard blue skies and desert-clear air. The countryside has an atmosphere that is rather more Far West than Middle West.

2. The village of Holcomb stands on the high wheat plains of western Kansas, a lonesome area that other Kansans call "out there." Some seventy miles east of the Colorado border, the countryside, with its hard blue skies and desert-clear air, has an atmosphere that is rather more Far West than Middle West.

   —*Truman Capote, In Cold Blood*

All questions of esthetics aside, Capote's writing is easier to read than is my mangling of it.

Thus, in the workshop, we do pay considerable attention to syntax. However, we are aware that at times convoluted, hard-to-read sentences and choppy prose serve a valid rhetorical purpose. (One of our mottoes is this: "Whatever works works.") We have no absolutes.

It is axiomatic that all native speakers of the language have total syntactic competence. In other words, they have the ability to use all of the structures of the language:

participial phrases,

> Anyone *wishing to communicate with America* should do so by e-mail, which has been specially invented for the purpose, *involving neither physical proximity nor speech.* (Auberon Waugh)

infinitive phrases,

> Obedience is better than sacrifice, and *to listen to God* is better than the fat of rams. (1 Samuel 15:22)

adjective clauses,

> That man is little to be envied *whose patriotism would not gain force upon the plain of Marathon,* or *whose piety would not grow warmer among the ruins of Iona.*(Samuel Johnson)

noun clauses,

> *What people call insincerity* is simply a method by which we can multiply our personalities. (Oscar Wilde)

and even nominative absolutes

> *The vote having been taken,* Cardinal Ratzinger became Pope Benedict XVI.

Introduction

Given that every native speaker of English has the *competence* to use the full resources of English syntax, the problem is activating this competence in *performance,* that is, encouraging writers to *use* what they know.

A comment on stylistic problems in one piece of writing from the workshop:

> Many problems with a writer's style—perhaps most problems—relate to the way in which the mind processes language. For instance, our world knowledge makes the following sentence perfectly comprehensible: *Standing on one leg in the swamp, I saw the heron.* Because of the structure of this sentence, however, readers must pause momentarily to reprocess the meaning. The so-called "dangling verbal" impedes the reading for a fraction of a second.
>
> Such is also the case with so-called "vague reference." Note the pronoun in the second sentence of your second paragraph: *It was fun letting **them** out. . . .* The reader must pause momentarily to determine the reference of *them. It was fun to let the birds out. . . .*

Several writers I have known in the workshops have developed unique *nonstandard* styles of their own. I am reluctant to urge them to adopt canons of Edited Standard English because their idiosyncrasies are part of the charm of their writing. If the style and register of a participant's writing are basically Edited Standard English, then deviations are glaring and should be eliminated. For example, Participant 6 writes, "Even the warmth of the cat's greeting, curling around her ankles and meowing softly, had no affect." In the context of Participant 6's relatively formal style, the substitution of *affect* for *effect* is a glaring lapse. On the other hand, here is a sample of the style of Participant 9:

> One bright rather sunny Fall Saturday morning, a sort of "Cajun Summer" day, We Seminarians and some of the Monks were invited to take a hike along this exceptional creek to a special outing terminating at an estate of one of our affluent neighbors to the north. There must have been 40 or so boys and 5 or 6 Monks. We split up roughly as ½ walked on the narrow asphalt road that followed the westerly edge of this stream and the rest of us electing to slosh along in the salubrious, pleasantly cool water flowing surprisingly slow, and enjoy the feel of crystal white sand under our feet and between our toes.

I feel, and the participants agree, that it would destroy the tone of Participant 9's written "voice" to regularize his style. The idiosyncrasies of capitalization and punctuation and the stumbling syntax are simply part of what we all think is a fascinating and moving autobiographical narrative.

Introduction

INVENTION

Every workshop participant has plenty to say—a lifetime of experience to tell us about. The problem is getting some participants to say it. For example, a lawyer has spent her career writing briefs and other legal documents, but now she wants to express herself in fiction, in a novel that is a sublimated record of her own professional life. The real problem that she has is coming from the abstraction of legal concepts to the concreteness of scenes, characters, and actions; in other words, the lawyer must become a dramatist.

Just the other day, we were reading a chapter from a novel by a retired engineer, a tale that has engaged all of us; we look forward to each installment. But in this case, I had a criticism. The writer gave extended descriptions of memorable scenery. My reaction was something like this: "You have a blank stage. The setting is beautiful, but I want characters to be doing something within that setting or against that background." (Interestingly, virtually all of the other members of the workshop group disagreed with me and were perfectly happy with the descriptive passages.)

Encouraging writers of narrative—whether fictional or autobiographical—to get down to cases, to bring characters to life, to make actions significant, in other words, to pack the writing with meaningful details—is the simplest concept and for some writers the most difficult task. But prompts from readers do achieve their purpose. "Give me more detail about the cabin." "What kind of frosting was on the cake?" "You write that the old man looked strange. What made you think this? What did he say or do? What did he wear?"

Here, for instance, are my comments on two pieces submitted in the workshop:

What would this fascinating tale be like if it were turned into a movie?

Well, we'd *see* St. Agnes School and *hear* the sounds that the children made. We might *smell* chalk dust or disinfectant.

We'd get to know Angela. We'd *see* her and *hear* her talk. Certainly we'd get more of the symptoms of her depression. (For example, *It seems that Angela never did raise her eyes from the floor. She walked as if in a trance, her sox sagging about her ankles, and her skirt stained with the stew that she had been served at lunch, but hadn't eaten.*)

Her mother. . . . Sister Veronica. . . .

But you have an advantage over Spielberg because you can know what's going on in the minds of your characters, or at least you can speculate about their thoughts and feelings. (If it's fiction, you can read minds. If it's not fiction, you can only infer and guess.)

Chapter 7 reads more like a newspaper report than a fictionalized account. It's the facts, sir, nothing but the facts. In a story, events have meaning only insofar as they relate to characters. For example, have Nhon experience and react to the bombing.

  Nhon could hear the approaching rumble of the engines as the B-52s neared the camp. He prepared himself for the thunder that would come when the planes, now shining silver streaks in the sky, released their bombs. He knew from experience that he would curl into a fetal position in his foxhole, his hands covering his ears.

Chapter 8 is a story, with (1) characters, (2) their actions and reactions, (3) the scenes in which the actions and reactions take place, and (4) the reasons for these actions and reactions.

CRITIQUES

Workshop participants very quickly become skilled critics/teachers of writing. As we read texts, we either understand or don't understand, become engaged or grow bored, are moved or repelled. In other words, we react intellectually or emotionally and thus have the basis for giving the writer useful responses. Not having the self-confidence or vocabulary necessary to respond to their colleagues' writing, participants are, in the first few workshop sessions, reluctant, but as the members of the group get to know and trust one another, and as they learn the sorts of responses (develop the vocabularies and tactics) that are helpful, they begin to participate in lively discussions that proceed on the basis of two assumptions:

First, responses will be specific, not general. The vapid comment such as "This is interesting" is taboo in the workshop and is replaced by "This is interesting specifically because. . . ." Every response must be accompanied by a pointatable.

Second, arguing about the validity of the responses is futile. If I told you that I don't like avocados, you wouldn't firmly respond, "Yes, you do!" If for some reason the text doesn't "work" for a reader, the process is, first, for the reader to explain the problem as he or she sees it and, second, for the writer to act on the suggestion or simply ignore it. A story that I repeatedly tell is this. My sister-in-law, whom I love dearly, wrote short stories, and she'd send them to me for my reactions. In my response to one of Boo's stories, I said something like this: "Well, I was really engaged until the very ending, but then you wrenched the whole plot from what was obviously going to be tragedy and made it into a happy Hollywood conclusion. I really didn't like the way you ended your story." Boo responded, "It's my story, and I'll end it any damn way I please." Wonderful! She taught me a great lesson, one that I use in my work with senior-citizen writers.

[The writer tells about sneaking a ride on a horse when she was a child.]

You're a good story-teller, largely because you set the scene: the hot concrete on bare feet, the thistle down wafting around you.

Molly is the most vivid character in the tale (the taffy-colored mane, the eyelashes). How about some of the details that characterize Billy and Hubert?

[This writer is creating a fantasy—a creation myth. Reading her story, one thinks of *The Hobbit* or *The Chronicles of Narnia*.]

I'm at a loss for comments. You certainly weave a mystic tapestry in this piece. And perhaps a reader should simply follow along, unquestioningly, uncritically. Yet you create so many problems that *this* reader becomes frustrated. For instance, you tell me that I should remember the inhabitants of the kingdoms, but that's a virtual impossibility—unless I memorize them by rote. But to what purpose?

Then I ask myself at times, "Is she playing with language, or has she misspelled?" For example (p. 2): These mortals, though illusive from human eyes. . . . *Illusive* is synonymous with *illusory*, and *illusory* means "based on or producing illusion," and an *illusion* is an optical or intellectual delusion or misapprehension. So something might be illusive *to* human eyes, but not from human eyes.

Of course, you might well be punning, *illusive* as word play with *elusive* (hard to comprehend or define).

I go on at length here simply to help you understand what you, the writer, are asking of me, the reader. These are but two examples.

On the other hand, I can think of a different kind of reading, one that simply drifts with the tale, glimpsing vistas through the mist.

You do demand a great deal of your readers, but, then, so did James Joyce.

Obviously, I don't have time to do a detailed response to your work. Such an endeavor would demand hours and hours every week. So I merely encourage you to keep writing without expecting that I'll do more than make a general comment or two.

[This autobiographical piece tells of the writer's boyhood in Scotland during World War II and of his starting work as an apprentice mechanic.]

Fascinating! One of the most interesting pieces I've read in many a moon. I could point to detail after detail, each of which is informative and dramatic. The tapes on the windows. The mobile anti-aircraft guns. The fetid shelters. Even the walk to the Nellie.

I think of *Angela's Ashes* or, better yet, *Sons and Lovers*. You could do something like this.

Introduction

Rewriting

As a teacher of writing at Carbon College in Utah, University of Kansas, University of Utah, University of Montana, and University of Southern California, I always found it difficult to get my students to revise their work; they inevitably viewed their first drafts as finished drafts. Such has not been the case with seniors in my workshops. They are avid revisers. (Not, of course, that every piece of writing needs revision or is worth revising.)

A simple rubric can serve as a handy reminder about rewriting and also as a guide to the sorts of responses one can make to texts. Namely, in revising/rewriting, one can perform only four operations.

> *Addition.* The writer can add words, phrases, sentences paragraphs. . . .
> *Deletion.* The writer can delete words, phrases, sentences, paragraphs. . . .
> *Rearrangement.* The writer can rearrange phrases, sentences, paragraphs. . . .
> *Substitution.* The writer can substitute one word, phrase, sentence, paragraph . . . for another.

A Word about Genres—and "Creativity"

In the workshops that I direct, the term "creative writing" is taboo, for the simple reason that all writing is creative, even drafting a proposal for funding or a set of instructions for assembling a complicated device. "Creative writing" means fictional narratives, dramas, and poems and excludes all of the genres of "referential" writing: biography, history, autobiography, argument, and persuasion. I have argued elsewhere[3] that the false dichotomy creative-noncreative resulting from Romantic theory in the nineteenth century (with Coleridge as the primary culprit) decimated and desiccated the literary canon that made up the subject matter of English departments in the United States and made possible the whole concept of "creative writing."

Writers as readers respond usefully to fiction and exposition and satire and autobiography. There is no practical reason for specifying a given genre in a writing workshop.

However, I discourage participants from submitting poetry, the reason being my own difficulty in responding to many of the "poems" that participants have submitted during the past years. I don't know how to react usefully and sympathetically to formless outpourings of emotion, the nature of much of the poetry that I have received.

The Role of the Workshop Leader

One of my former graduate students from the University of Southern California recently asked me, "I wonder . . . whether that philosophy of yours about cultivating 'happy anarchy' in the classroom applies [to the workshops for seniors]?" My answer was, "Emphatically yes!" As the leader-facilitator of the workshops, my role is just to keep the talk going (though, in the process, I probably talk too much). The talk in the workshops flows naturally through the terrain laid out by the texts that are being discussed. Upon occasion, when I think that such talk will be useful, I intrude my English-teacher self with information about such matters as syntactic fluency (i.e., sentence structure) and my own quiddities such as the distinction between *its* and *it's*.

It's extremely important that participants view the workshop leader as a writer. Thus, I submit, for the scrutiny of the group, examples of stuff I've published and of ongoing work.

NUTS-AND-BOLTS

1. Fifteen is the absolute upper limit for the number of workshop participants. Any number greater than fifteen makes it impossible for all of the participants to have their say.
2. I have found that two hours is the optimum period for each meeting.
3. At each meeting, every participant gives copies of his or her work to the others in the group and to me. These submissions are the basis for the next session's discussion.
4. School districts often have adult education programs that can sponsor writing workshops for seniors. The Emeriti College at University of Southern California has sponsored some of the workshops I have conducted. Community senior centers are another source of sponsorship.

Notes

[1] According to the year 2000 census, of the 281 million Americans, some 54 million were age 55 or older, as compared with 38 million college-age Americans.

[2] George Hillocks, Jr. "Rhetoric in Classrooms: Prospects for the Twenty-First Century." James D. Williams, ed. *Visions and Revisions: Continuity and Change in Rhetoric and Composition.* Carbondale: Southern Illinois UP, 2002. 219–46.

[3] *A Teacher's Introduction to Composition in the Rhetorical Tradition.* Urbana: NCTE, 1994 (37–43); *The English Department: A Personal and Institutional History.* Carbondale: Southern Illinois UP, 1998 (101–183).

[4] I am substituting impersonal numberings for the actual names of the participants.

[5] Since I want participants to view me as a writer, as a member of the group, each week I submit a sample of my own writing: fiction, exposition, history, autobiography.

Appendix: Example Handout

Oct. 11, 2005

Participant 1[4]

Wonderful tale. Give it more horsepower.

Joe was the star of the show. He used a mop for a wig and oranges in his brassiere to give himself oomph. His white skirt with large pink polka dots was perhaps a size six,

and it barely covered his ample overhang. .
. .

Joe, Bill, and I did a chorus of "Sweet Ade-
line," each of us taking swigs of ice tea from a
brown jug. Our harmony might not have been
perfect, but we put real heart into that song.

Participant 2

What would this fascinating tale be like if it were
turned into a movie?

Well, we'd *see* St. Agnes School and *hear* the sounds
that the children made. We might *smell* chalk dust or
disinfectant.

We'd get to know Angela. We'd *see* her and *hear* her
talk. Certainly we'd get more of the symptoms of her
depression. (*It seems that Angela never did raise her eyes
from the floor. She walked as if in a trance, her sox sagging about her ankles, and her skirt stained with the stew
that she had been served at lunch, but hadn't eaten.*)

Her mother. . . . Sister Veronica. . . .

But you have an advantage over Spielberg because you
can know what's going on in the minds of your characters, or at least you can speculate about their thoughts
and feelings. (If it's fiction, you can read minds. If it's
not fiction, you can only infer and guess.)

Theda, take a look at Michelle's stuff.

Participant 3

P. 6, 2ⁿᵈ par. Wonderful.

I won't go into detail, but, as usual, I think this stuff
is really wonderful. But. . . .

P. 6. New paragraph at "Her mother put on her
apron. . . ."

P. 9. Transition essential. Also, more development. Or simply a gap. Or even double spacing to indicate a major shift. IN FACT, just delete the last paragraph on p. 9. That's *not* a suggestion. It's an *order*.

Participant 4

I suspect you're doing family history—or your husband's family history. Am I right? If so, you tell the story as if it were fiction; thus, you've created a cameleopard. The piece is well done as *fiction,* but if it is fiction, your contract with the reader is quite different from the non-fiction contract. If it's fiction, you can do anything you want: read minds, have *deus ex machina,* let Janchi escape in a rocket ship. If it's not fiction, you must play it straight. You can speculate about what characters might be thinking. And so on. Your stance as the omniscient narrator invalidates this as history. (And maybe it isn't history. I don't know.) For a discussion of this problem, see W. Ross Winterowd, *The Rhetoric of the Other Literature* (Carbondale: Southern Illinois UP, 1990).

Participant 5

Your tenses still skitter. For example, see p. 7.

David isn't believable. PhD at 16. Founds a department at 17. The guy might be the world's greatest genius, but he still must go through the academic mill.

Your introductions to direct quotes become tics. "Maria bluntly. . . ." "Lupe pointedly. . . ."

One virtue: the information about obsidian and so forth that you provide the reader.

Another virtue: the suspense you build into the plot. Well done. Kidnapping? Human sacrifice? The inevitable warming up of the toluca.

Participant 6

Charming tale. Part fantasy, part history. I suppose. Once again, my five-year-old would like the story—and would learn from it.

Participant 7

Your first paragraph catches me.

"The cat stretched like pulled taffy. . . ." Wonderful!!!

P. 5. affect/effect

Can a cat and a bird be astonished? My cat is utterly stupid, and she's among the more intelligent cats in town.

A touching story. I think you'd have more horsepower if we got to know Florence and Sue better. One way you could accomplish this definition would be to expand on the scene in which they tell one another their stories. Use dialogue. *Show* their emotions by what they say and do.

Suggestion: work on this one. It has great potential.

Participant 8

I greatly enjoy the background that you provide: the landscape, the food, the customs. Perhaps you move a bit too rapidly from scene to scene. I diffidently suggest that you could strengthen your tale if you'd give your scenes more depth. Details. Dialogue. Gestures.

Participant 9

Delicious fruit. So? Peaches? Pears? Bananas?

Finger foods. So? Cucumber sandwiches? Paté? Pickled herring?

Endless desserts. So? Chocolate éclairs? Apple pie? Tapioca pudding. Green Jell-O with shredded carrots and topped with Miracle Whip?

In "Hike and Picnic," you're not at your best, but you regain your touch in "Muralist," "Fasting," and "Choir."

As usual, I enjoy the warm humanity that your stuff radiates.

[As an example of what I mean by providing detail, I wrote the following. A good rule of thumb of is "tell and then *show*."] My Great-Aunt Dolly indulged me beyond reason and measure. I remember the chocolate éclairs, with their gooey custard filling, their bittersweet chocolate icing, and their flaky crusts. She took me to the day-old bakery to pick out treats, and I particularly liked the greasy cake donuts, which I could dunk in milk or tea. Peppermint lozenges— an endless supply. And ice cream—the two of us sharing a quart. And when, finally, my stomach ached because of Aunt Dolly's indulgence, she gave me paregoric, so aromatic and sweet that the stomach ache was worth the remedy. (By the way, paregoric is camphorated tincture of opium. Because of Aunt Dolly, I was a child junky.)

Participant 9

The craftsmanship here is admirable. For instance, the first long paragraph (pp. 19–20)—Hemingway couldn't have done better. (Or Matthiessen, whom I prefer to Hemingway.)

The Sermon as Cop-Out[5]

W. Ross Winterowd

I recently listened to a sermon the theme of which was fidelity to one's commitments. The Genesis story of Joseph and Potiphar's wife was the text on which the pastor anchored the moral of his homily. After all, Biblical truths are mere truisms until they are brought to life with some episode, a concrete situation, as was the case in the sermon that I recently heard. We remember that Potiphar's wife tried to seduce Joseph, but Joseph rebuffed her, saying, "Look, with me here, my master has no concern about anything in the house, and he has put everything that he has in my hand. He is not greater in the house than I am, nor has he kept back anything from me except yourself, because you are his wife. How then could I do this great wickedness, and sin against God?"

Biblical dramas are powerful, carrying as they do the weight of tradition and, for most congregations, the authority of God. Furthermore, they are simply good stories; the Bible is wonderful literature. However, there are dramas outside the Bible and outside the exempla that preachers draw from sources such as *Reader's Digest* or *One Minute Wisdom,* by Anthony de Mello.

As I scan the front page of today's *Los Angeles Times* (May 11, 2005), I find these dramas pertaining to fidelity to one's commitments: "UNITED AIRLINES CLEARED TO SHED PENSION PLANS. A bankruptcy judge allows the carrier to transfer $6.6 billion of liabilities to a U.S. agency. Some retirees' benefits may be affected"; "A GLIMPSE AT THE MIND OF A PEDOPHILE. A former priest who served under Mahony in the Stockton Diocese describes his ploys"; "EXPERTS ARE AT A LOSS ON INVESTING. Nobel winners and top academics fumble the sorts of decisions Bush's Social Security overhaul plan would ask average Americans to make."

Pastors have a wonderful opportunity to segue from moral truism to Biblical exemplum to the drama of real world issues simply by asking congregations to consider how the principle illustrated by scriptural passages applies to the quotidian dramas of our very troubled age. I would even suggest that by organizing discussion groups pastors could bring new energy to their congregations: groups that within the walls of the chapel or church would use Biblical wisdom as the starting point for discussions of here-and-now ethical issues.

I have closely followed the contentious religious issues that currently seem to preoccupy at least a large segment of the Christian community: the phrase "under God" in the pledge; the Ten Commandments in courtrooms and on city or state property; more significantly, same-sex marriage; and, most significantly, right to life. The perhaps most powerful clergy in these debates strip these issues of their nuances and hence reduce moral and political controversies to the truism of either-or, black-or-white. For example, I am ardently in the so-called "right-to-life" camp, and that being the case, I am appalled by the ardor with which clergy such as Lou Sheldon and Jerry Falwell oppose abortion *without* acknowledging the fact that among developed nations, the United States has the highest rate of infant mortality. The Centers for Disease Control and Prevention reports that "The United States ranked 28th in the world in infant mortality in 1998. This ranking is due in large part to disparities which continue to exist among various racial and ethnic groups in this country, particularly African Americans." And Falwell's now famous rant about 9/11:

> The abortionists have got to bear some burden for this because God will not be mocked. And when we destroy 40 million little innocent babies, we make God mad. I really believe that the pagans, and the abortionists, and the feminists, and the gays and the lesbians who are actively trying to make that an alternative lifestyle, the ACLU, People for the American Way, all of them who have tried to secularize America, I point the finger in their face and say: you helped this happen.

Pastors have a wonderful opportunity to engage folks in the kind of dialogue that is the motive for *moral* action in the here-and-now, and of what use is morality if it is not active? Is "abstract morality" an oxymoron?

You see what I'm getting at. Grounding truisms in Biblical episodes is safe. I have the sense that congregations listen to the sermons, recite the doxology, bow their heads for the final prayer, and leave the church uplifted and cleansed. But I know enough about myself and my fellow mortals to understand that we need more than moral uplift to take action. I would like to find a congregation in which sermons led to intense discussions about the Iraq mess, about the degradation of the environment, about the increasing gap between the haves and the have-nots, and about other festering problems that will face those about whose future I care most: my grandchildren. I know that there are such congregations, but I haven't yet found them.

WORKS CITED

700 Club. Christian Broadcasting Network. 13 Sept. 2001.

Center for Disease Control Office of Minority Health. 2006 (10 October 2006) <http://www.cdc.gov/omh/AMH/factsheets/infant.htm>.

Michelle Barany

I am a retired French instructor who, in addition to teaching French in colleges and at a university, also majored in English, Creative Writing Option. After my retirement, under my husband's and children's promptings (one son and two daughters), as well as that of the instructor in the senior workshop I recently attended, I compiled six short stories, one essay and two novellas into a collection entitled: Far from the Shade of the Pepper Tree.

These stories are autobiographical, revisiting my childhood in France before and during World War II. They are in the voice of Janine, my alter ego. They often shuttle between the American and the French shores and between the past and the present of the story.

This is an excerpt from an autobiographical short story, "Homeward."

The story takes place in the late 1960s. Janine is from France. Married to her American husband, Dan, she is living in California with their three children and is on her way to a California State University, where she teaches French. Her own classes over, she attends a Short Story Writing class at the same university, has a short story to write, doesn't know what to write about and considers what could make

up a complete story. She would also like to return to France
for a visit but knows that, with young children at home, it
may take a few years.

Homeward (Excerpt)

After she entered the North 405 freeway, she
switched to the left lane to avoid the on-ramp traffic.
She caught up with a convoy of army trucks with their
lights on, moving in the right lane at a slower pace than
the speed limit. They might be soldiers preparing for
their tour of duty in Vietnam, she thought.

It had been a long time since she had last seen such
a convoy. Not since she had left France perhaps; and
there, some twenty years ago, passing between the pop-
lars or the oaks bordering the narrow French highways,
they had meant deliverance.

As she drove past the trucks, she could not see the
drivers, just an elbow on the edge of a window and part
of a hand on part of a steering wheel, then for a few
seconds, a face framed in the steel rim of a side mirror,
still as if within a rippleless pool.

In preparation for her cut off to the university, she
slowed down to let the trucks pass her. Ahead and behind, in the lane next to hers, the convoy unfurled.
And involuntarily, she kept her eyes averted because
of that other convoy of trucks and tanks, preceded by
motorcycles and mounted soldiers, German this time,
passing the bus she was in, in June of 1940 when they
came into Niort, about three hundred kilometers west
of Paris.

Janine had been living with her aunt Alice during that year because Niort was thought to be safer than Paris where her maternal grandparents lived, or Gap close to the Italian boundary, where her parents had moved from Paris a few years earlier.

Unstopped, unchallenged, the Germans had come to Niort on their journey west. School being let out in June that year instead of the traditional fourteenth of July, Aunt Alice was taking Janine to her aunt Marie in La Rochelle, where her uncle would take both Janine and his daughter Danielle to their grandmother's home in the small village of Les Fougères, 20 kilometers away.

The bus moved very slowly as the German soldiers approached it from behind. In the street, every house's shutters were closed, every store's iron blinds drawn. And the refugees who, for the past month had come in droves from Belgium and from the eastern provinces of France by foot and who, in their dark clothing, had lined the streets on either side like black edges on death notices, had fled, Janine did not know where.

From behind the bus, she could hear the puttering of motors, the drumming of hooves. From the corner of her eyes, she glanced at the other passengers. Their heads were erect but their eyes lowered. No one paid attention to Janine, including tall, blond Aunt Alice.

Janine turned her head slowly toward the window and flattened her nose against the glass to see what the enemy looked like. He was approaching on horseback. Her eyes rose slowly from the black boots in shining stirrups, along the pepper green uniform, past the wide belt with the black holster, the dark cape thrown back like a Roman warrior's, to the magisterial face. Her eyes met his. Curious, unwavering, she stared. He stared back. She kept staring. He screwed up his nose and stuck his tongue out. Startled, she looked away. Surely her imagination had played a trick on her! She looked again to make sure. And again he stuck out his tongue.

She forgot he was the conqueror. Bewildered and indignant, she tapped her aunt's hand. "Aunt Alice, the German stuck his tongue out at me!"

"Sit still," Aunt Alice said. "And don't look back."

"But he stuck his tongue out at me!"

Aunt Alice glanced from beneath her lashes, a quick, furtive glance, barely moving her eyelids.

"Do not look back," she repeated, insisting. "And most of all *do not* stick your tongue out at him."

Janine wanted to glance once more, but her aunt's tone, even though barely more than a whisper, cautioned that one couldn't tell what a soldier might do. Janine couldn't very well disobey. Not with her aunt facing her. Twisting in her seat, she turned her head ever so slightly toward the street, then kept it erect, as the horses' hooves kept their steady rhythmic pounding closer to the rear of her window. From the corner of her eyes, she could now see the mounted soldier towering above her on the other side of the window. Was he still watching her? She raised her eyes in an upward slant to check and met his, sternly staring down at her. She sat very still now, her eyes averted until the column enfolding the bus had passed.

She hadn't recalled the German episode in ages. She wouldn't have, had she not caught up with the convoy of American soldiers. It could be something to write about, she thought; but immediately she dismissed the idea. It was an anecdote. Not a complete story.

The trucks were disappearing on the freeway behind the foliage lining her cut off, and the Humanities Tower on upper campus loomed tall in the near distance.

***

At the university, as she taught her classes then attended the Short Story Writing class conducted by Dr. Cory, she tried several ideas on as possible subjects for the story she had to write but dismissed them. Upon leaving the university, she paused to reflect on a cryptic sculpture whose many diverging branches seemed to lead nowhere.

That evening, back at her desk at home, the children in bed and her husband teaching evening classes at a community college, she faced her typewriter. She leafed through the "next to nothing" notebook that Dan had given her. She found a paragraph she had once written in longhand on, of all things, the peach trees that Dr. Cory, in the writing class, had mentioned, saying that some of his students ought to do something with them, put them in a story. She retyped the paragraph: "At the university, the petals of peach trees offered a gamut of pink, intricately painted. When they began to fade, the lavender blue of jacarandas replaced them, the windblown flowers beneath mirroring like a pool the broad canopy above. Today the Santa Ana winds swept them away."

She stopped. Read the paragraph. Read it again. She changed the word windblown to fallen. Now what? To pick up momentum, she retyped the whole paragraph in the future tense, changing today to to-morrow. But when she typed the last period, again it was a *point final*. Dead end. What more could one say about peach blossoms? Jacarandas? Perhaps it was not what Dr. Cory had meant. Not literally.

Sensing a presence behind her, she pushed her chair away from her desk, turned around. In his pajamas Scotty was standing, watching her type. She had not heard him come up. She knew something was on his mind. She often stayed longer with the children than she had tonight, talking problems over, reading a story with them in English, singing a song in French.

"What's up?" she asked, pulling her son onto her lap.

"If you and Dad were gone, would I still be able to talk with you?"

"What do you mean," she asked to give herself time to think.

He had asked her before where her mother was, why she never called Aunt Marie or Uncle Charles in La Rochelle. Her arm around his shoulder, she led him to his room.

He stopped midway, turned to her, insistent. "If you weren't around any more, could I still be with you? Could I hear you if you talked to me?"

She was not prepared for the question, for an answer he would accept because he meant dead. If she were dead.

In his bedroom, she raised the cover on his bed. He slid under. She sat next to him. She explained about the body having to be put away, about the soul remaining. She stopped. Perhaps his father could have done better.

"But would you be able to talk with me?" he insisted. "Would I hear you?"

"Somehow," she said. "You would. You'd think of us. Remember. Hear us."

"Remember as when you call me, 'Your cubby. Or when I climbed the rocks with Dad at Joshua Tree and hid and you stayed behind and said. . . . '"

"Like that," she said.

He squeezed her hand. She kept his between hers. Even when he fell asleep, she stayed. Talk to him? Yes, she could. Forever. Her mother, Uncle Charles, Aunt Marie . . . They talked. All the time. In the way she prepared a meal, remembered a bit of advice, handled a situation.

Scotty may have understood intuitively what she had tried to say. She did not know. She laid his hand carefully on the bed. She pulled the quilt over his shoulders.

She returned upstairs, sat at the typewriter. She turned the current on, set the carriage in place.

"After her mother had died in August 1940," Janine began typing, "she carried with her wherever she went, in her pocket during the day, under her pillow at night, a flat silver box which had once contained candy. In it were a picture of her parents together and a small *bonne année* card her mother had sent her the previous year. Sitting at the table next to her cousin, Danielle, in Aunt Marie's dining room, she did her homework conscientiously so that her mother, even though dead, would be pleased. She felt the silver box in her pocket. Behind her, the coal stove that Aunt Marie had lit earlier began to burn, and a warm stream rose along her back.

"It was Sunday. Madeleine, an employee of Aunt Marie, who preferred spending her days off at Aunt Marie's than with her remarried mother, half sisters and step-dad came in ready to accompany Danielle and Janine on a walk. That Sunday, Madeleine took them to an attraction park where they watched the rides of people in bumper cars being bumped and pursuing others. It looked like fun. When the ride stopped, a car glided along the side next to them, and a handsome German officer offered his hand to Madeleine to invite her for a ride with him. Madeleine took a step forward then shaking her head to decline moved backward, and probably because Janine at ten was the younger of the two cousins, she pushed her toward the officer in the car instead of taking his hand herself. Janine had heard that an elite of the German army had been sent to France to befriend the population. Indeed, the officer with a mature expression on his perhaps thirty-year-old face, handsome in a well fitting, impeccable uniform looked kind and correct and acted accordingly. He spoke French and asked Janine what grade she was in at school. Shy and feeling awkward, she answered in monosyllables. When the ride finished and she stepped out of the car, the officer held his hand toward Danielle to help her in, in turn. But this time, as Danielle was about to step into the car, Madeleine suddenly held her back and, sidestepping her, got into the car instead. The officer smiled. Madeleine blushed. Her face remained flushed, Janine noticed, for the rest of the ride.

"When it stopped, she got out of the car as fast as if a bomb had been dropped on the recreation park and debris were about to fall on her. Barely acknowledging the officer with a brief nod, her face scarlet red, she grabbed Danielle's and Janine's hands and pulling them along swept out of the attraction park, making them promise not to ever, ever tell anyone, especially not Mr. Mallet, Janine's Uncle Charles. Not because the young man was a German, but because in those days, he was the enemy and she was loyal. From that day on, she passed any German in the street, erect, looking straight ahead. Madeleine at eighteen. . . .

"Back at Aunt Marie's, Uncle Charles, who had already joined the underground Resistance, came down from his workshop to listen to the BBC news broadcast. He sat at the head of the table, his large beret slanting far down his cheek. The angrier he was, the more his beret slanted. Ever since the formation of the Vichy Government and its collaboration with Hitler, the beret slanted more and more. . . ."

Like the diverging yet intricately linked branches of the metal sculpture at the university, a profusion of anecdotes, their memory still sharp despite the mist of time, pulled her in every direction: Janine and her mother in 1939, the two of them running together through the streets of Paris to find and buy Janine blue and white shoes like her mother's that last Easter before the war. . . . Her father in Gap in 1937 who, when Janine was sick, made paper hens and baby chicks for her, so that she could pretend that the baby chicks got lost in the valleys of maroon pillows on the dining-room divan bed, where during the day she rested to get well, while her mother read on a chair by the bay window and the snow fell outside. . . . Her school friend, Monique Picot, motherless like Janine in the La Rochelle of 1941, who held Janine's hand back when Janine inadvertently drew Crosses of Lorraine, General De Gaulle's symbol, on the ice frosted window of their classroom, while the students waited in line for a monitor to come in and dismiss the class.

"Attention, Janine. It's dangerous," Monique had said, adding with a smile, "It's too soon yet." She was right, one did not know who could be trusted, classmate or teacher. Monique, killed, along with her three sisters and the governess her widowed father was soon to marry, in a bombing of St-Etienne, a town in the Creusot Mountains, where her father had sent them when all the children had to be evacuated from La Rochelle. . . .

Under Janine's fingers, the keys pounded. The words arose as if conjured up. People from times gone surged forward, talking, gesturing, free again, released from the confines of her mind, talking to her from her childhood in blessed ignorance of the story form. But along the sheet on the roller, along chestnut and broom-lined paths, past weather-beaten crosses and heather-covered hills, they were leading her, taking her home, on a journey home.

Into the Night of Time

May 7

Dear Elisse,

I enjoyed your phone call, Honey. You say that you have to make a report about history? You will have to present it before your fifth-grade class? And you have chosen me, your French maternal grandmother, as your subject?

I am flattered. I didn't realize before that I was a part of history, but upon reflection, I suppose I am. After all, I do go back to a pre-World-War-II-era, and . . . Oh, no, you said, not that history. Family history, the kind which, in the old-fashioned way, was handed down from generation to generation through stories. And the story you heard me tell your cousin Keith once has to do with one of those thin flexible branches, called switches, that were used ever so lightly on the back of the legs of misbehaving children. You said that it had to do with a switch that, as a child, I tried to get rid of.

I don't remember that. What I do remember is a bouquet of the thin branches, a bouquet of switches, tied together by a beautiful bow. I found it on a Christmas morning inside a brand new doll carriage that the Père Noël, as the French children call Santa Claus, had brought me.

I guess he wanted to tell me that I owed the carriage to his generosity but should watch out and be more obedient in the future.

You said I couldn't possibly have deserved the switches, that your grandma could only be a good girl. Well, I'll let you be the judge:

It begins way back, into the night of time.

It was the summer of 1935 and I was five years old. My parents were moving from Paris, France, to Gap, a city in the French Alps, for my mother's health. About two years earlier, my grandparents had also moved from Paris because of a period called the Depression. My grandfather lost his long-time job in Paris, and with my grandmother, went to Mazermaud, a village near Limoges, in the central part of France, where they had a big house and a very vast garden. In order to give my parents time to settle in their new city, and my mother a chance to get well, my grandmother came to Paris to pick me up and bring me back to live with her and my grandfather.

My grandmother had roses, snapdragons, tulips, pansies, and peonies growing all around the house and along edges enclosing my grandfather's vegetable patches. He grew peas, green beans, lettuces, potatoes, carrots and cabbages. He also raised rabbits and chickens. He had fenced in a long and wide area where hens and rooster pecked at the ground, strutted and clucked all day long. At the end of the garden were the rabbit cages. They were secured on four to five-foot-high piles hammered into the ground, and when I looked inside the cages through the grilled doors, my nose and the rabbits' noses would touch through the wire mesh.

When my grandfather worked in the garden and cleaned the rabbit cages, I watched him. When my grandmother fed the chickens, late in the afternoon, I followed her into the coop and watched. The chickens came running as soon as they saw her, stretching their necks toward her. They clucked indignantly, I thought, when in their chicken's opinion she took too long before throwing the grain on the ground. Then they rushed on the seeds my grandmother threw, each hen pecking at as many seeds as it could before the others did.

Most of the time, I was alone in the garden. I made up games, but when I grew tired of them, I tried to befriend the hens and visited them in their pen. But when they saw me, they didn't come running up to me as they did to my grandmother. They walked or ran away instead, stretching their necks righteously and clucking as if to say, "Look at her! She has no right to be here! Get out, you're bothering us!"

One evening, after my grandmother had thrown the grain over to the chickens and left, I lingered behind. The chickens were too busy eating as fast as they could to notice me. I tiptoed behind one of them and, bending over slowly, I grabbed it suddenly by the tail and held it up for a while. I didn't want to hurt it. I wanted to hear it cluck for a good reason. It did. Then I put it down and moved on to another one. Before long, the whole roost was clucking and my grandmother came running to see what had so disturbed the hens. She said

I was to let the poor chickens eat peacefully, and she forbade me to go into the chicken coop alone again.

My real friends were the rabbits. There was generally one per cage. One morning, after I was up, my grandfather said, "Come with me. Let's go see the rabbits." It wasn't the time he usually cleaned the cages or fed the rabbits. I followed him. And there, next to the mother rabbit were many baby rabbits, bumping around, halfway blind, to and from the mother rabbit's warm belly. Within a week, they had grown enough to come to the door and, through the grill, wiggle their noses under mine. I tried to see how many there were, but they hopped about so much inside the cage that it made it difficult for me to count them. Five. Six. More.

I danced for them and they watched through the grill. I talked to them and they listened, their faces sideways, their ears upright, one toward me. When I walked away, they huddled behind the door, envying my freedom, I thought.

I felt sorry for them. One day, I said, "You poor little rabbits. Wouldn't you like to be free like me outside in the big garden?" And their little noses went up and down, twitching faster than usual, saying, "Yes, yes, yes, we would like it very much."

I knew my grandfather was working in his workshop, building a kitchen cabinet for my grandmother. He wouldn't see me. I turned toward the house. My grandmother wasn't watching me through a window or through the panes on the kitchen door. I opened the cage and took out one little rabbit at a time. Now I could count them. There were nine.

I carried one and placed it beneath a big cabbage, another one between rows of carrots, another in the lettuce patch, yet another behind a cherry tree. I found a good hiding place for each of them. When I was finished, I closed the cage on the mother rabbit. She was much too big to carry out.

I don't remember exactly when my grandmother came to check what I was doing. But when she did, she saw one little rabbit hopping across the path in front of her. She checked the cage and immediately ran back toward the house to call for my grandfather's help. "Come see what your granddaughter has done this time," she said.

My grandparents spent the rest of the day looking for the rabbits (I wouldn't tell them where they were) and catching them. By evening, the rabbits were back in their cage, but I couldn't tell them how sorry I was that they had been caught because I was no more permitted by the rabbit cages than I was by the chicken coop.

Without chickens or rabbits, I was pretty lonely. On a very hot day, however, a boy about eight years old with very dark, wavy hair and a girl about four with long light brown hair came into the garden. They were Gypsy children, I could tell. They probably lived in a horse-drawn trailer that I had seen parked on the Village Square when my grandmother took me along shopping. The horse had been tied to a rail that encircled the square. Gypsies traveled all over France, some all over Europe, and they never stayed very long in any one place.

When the children came into the garden, I was pushing a stroller with a seat that always came loose and hung down, and carrying a doll which never smiled. I went running toward them. "You're coming to play with me," I said.

"No," the boy said. "We're coming to see your mother. Is she in?"

"Yes, she's in; but she's not my mother, she's my grandmother."

"It's all right," the boy said. "We want to know if she would have something to give us."

"Like what?"

"Pots and pans. Old rags."

"I don't think so. But you can ask her. Knock on the door. She'll answer."

I had always heard my grandmother say no, she didn't have anything, when grownup Gypsies came asking; but I had also seen her give them some *sous* (they were the equivalent of pennies), and the Gypsies were always pleased.

"Is she nice?" the boy asked.

"My grandmother? Mostly," I said. "But make sure you knock first even if the door is opened and wait till she says, 'Come in,' before you go in." Some Gypsies walked into the kitchen without knocking and my grandmother never gave them anything then.

The boy hesitated. "What about you," he said. "Do you have things you don't want?" The girl stayed close to him and never spoke.

"Like what? I don't have anything."

"Sure you do. You have toys. Like old toys."

I felt my eyes open wide. All of a sudden I knew. "I have this stroller and this doll. But the doll never smiles."

The boy's eyes grew wider and the little girl's too as she looked up at me. "Don't you want them?" he asked.

"You can have them."

I could see how pleased the children were and it made me feel good.

"But the doll never smiles and the stroller seat is loose."

"That's all right. I can fix it."

"You can?"

"Sure," he said. "With some twine, it's easy."

I was surprised because my grandfather had tried many times to repair it, but it always came apart. My new friends were so happy, though, that I was not about to argue. On the one hand, I was delighted to get rid of a stroller and of a doll that I never liked, but on the other hand, I felt guilty to give my new friends toys that I found to be bad. "I have a ball too. It's almost new," I offered.

The boy hesitated. He looked toward the kitchen. "No," he said. "This is enough."

The girl carried the doll and the boy started pushing the stroller toward the gate.

"You live in the trailer on the Village Square?" I asked.

The boy and the girl stopped. They nodded.

"And you can eat and sleep inside?"

"Yes."

There's a table? And a stove? And beds too?"

"Sure," he said. "Come with us and we'll show you."

"What will your mother say?"

"She won't mind."

"Is she nice?"

"Yes. Come on. She won't mind."

So then, I looked toward the kitchen to check and make sure that my grandmother was not watching from the doorstep. She was not, and the three of us left. The boy and I carried the stroller down the steps from the garden onto the village road. Then, the boy pushing the stroller and the girl carrying the doll, we ran down the road to where it sloped down a fairly long hill. I knew that if we quickly got to the bottom, my grandmother could not see us even if she started look-ing for me.

Running, I turned around. No one was in sight. I turned again. Still no one. As we neared the bottom of the hill, I turned once more. There, at the top, I saw the silhouette of my grandmother bobbing in the shim-mering heat. The boy had turned too. He saw her. We ran faster. The boy turned again. He stopped us from running. He pushed the stroller toward me, took the doll from his sister's arm and handed it to me. "We have to go," he said. "Your grandmother would think we stole your toys."

"No, she won't. I'll tell her I gave them to you. She'll believe me."

"We have to go," he said. He and his sister started on their way.

"My grandmother wouldn't scold me as much if you stayed with me." I could see her clearly now. In one hand she carried a switch.

The boy stopped. He looked back at me and at my grandmother. He grabbed his sister's hand and came to stand next to me.

My grandmother caught up with us. "I gave them the carriage and the doll. They are theirs. I want them to keep them," I told her.

She pushed the carriage closer to me, "Go on home," she said.

I could tell she wasn't pleased with me. But I waited.

She turned to the children. Her face now had a kinder expression. She handed a five-sous piece to each and spoke gently, "You two go on now."

I watched the children start on their way, but they immediately turned back, stood an instant and waved at me. Sniffling, I waved back. I sniffled all the way back home as I carried the doll which never smiled and pushed the carriage with the hanging seat all the way back up the hill. I wasn't sniffling because my grandmother scolded me; she did not. Not because the switch stung my legs; it did not. My grandmother never used it. I cried because the children were not allowed to keep the toys that had made them so happy and because I had lost my friends so soon after meeting them.

When Christmas Eve came that year and I placed my shoes before the fireplace, I was very worried that

Père Noël would not bring me anything. But "he" did, a smiling doll and a beautiful doll carriage with, in the center, a bouquet of switches tied with a big red bow.

This is the end of my story. It is now up to you, my dear little granddaughter, to decide whether your grandma deserved this warning from the Père Noël.

Love,
Grandmother

Rooftops

The first deafening roar of the war sirens caught ten-year-old Janine unaware on a rooftop four stories above ground. She always came to the roof through an attic bay window of her Aunt Marie and Uncle Charles' house, where she had lived since her mother's death last August.

Every Thursday on her regular day off from school, she clambered out onto the roof to see La Rochelle from above as her mother might see it from Heaven, the pretty blue-slated roofs and the red-tiled ones, the scene pierced here and there by century-old steeples and turrets. She also wanted to show her eleven-year-old cousin Danielle, Aunt Marie and Uncle Charles' daughter, how far a skinny, wiry girl like herself was in reality walking on rooftops without hanging on to chimneys, passing open skylights without sliding into them, and walking on the edge of enclosed narrow courtyards without plummeting inside, because her mother's invisible hand holding hers kept her safe.

At the blaring of the sirens, she froze. Stared at the four black horns back to back, so monster-like even when they were silent. They wailed across the street from her, from the top of the Bonvent Boys School, now partially occupied by the German army as a branch of their headquarters.

It was the first alert since the Germans had come to La Rochelle last June when, Uncle Charles had told her after she had come to live with him and Aunt Marie, their goose steps had echoed through the paved streets of the town, filtered through the locked doors of the houses, through their closed shutters, the drawn shutters the mourning equivalent of the black clothes she wore now that her mother was dead, of the black band Uncle Charles wore on his lapel.

From other parts of town, other sirens joined in. It was a dirge, a black cloud of sounds, rising, falling over the town, all the way to the invisible ocean. She lost her balance and, her arms flailing, slid over several slates. She stopped back of the drain pipe as if, at the last moment, her mother's hand had held her back.

Her heart pounding, she turned around, and crouching, climbed back up the slant of this roof, down the side of that one, past the wide open skylight above the stairway of the apartment building where Uncle Charles' friend Mr. Khoeler lived, onto the roof of her aunt and uncle's house.

She reached the chimney facing the attic window, where Danielle, her hand as if paralyzed next to her open mouth, watched and waited for her. With her back against the cresting roof of the house next door, moving sideways, Janine made her way back along a narrow strip of slates bordering a glass-paned skylight. It stretched between the chimney and the attic window, closing a wide shaft punctuated way down by her aunt's baker's furnace. She reached the window just as her uncle's tall bulk, crowned by his large beret slanting down his cheek, surged beside his daughter. He grabbed Janine's arm and pulled her into the attic. Outside, the sirens were still wailing.

"To the basement," he said.

She would be accountable later, she knew, for her rooftop explorations. Until then, Danielle only had known of them. Janine rushed down the stairway after her. She heard her uncle lock the window behind them. Soon after, his footsteps hammered down the narrow steps.

She sensed, sometimes, when he ruffled the top of her head half-gruffly, half-affectionately after she had gotten into some mischief—a broken glass, a pressing request to have room on the busy table to do her home-work *now*—that he wondered what to make of this niece who had fallen to his and Aunt Marie's care.

Janine had been spending the summer months with Grandmother and Danielle in Les Fougères when the news of her mother's death had reached her. Coming to Les Fougères the following Sunday, it was Uncle Charles who, setting Janine on his lap, had asked her if she would come to live with him, with Aunt Marie and Danielle until the war was over and she could be reunited with her father. He could not leave Gap, the city in the unoccupied part of France where he and her mother had lived just before the war. Sometimes, though, she felt as if there were territories where she could not trespass, because they had already been claimed by Uncle Charles for Danielle.

Rushing downstairs, past the open door to Uncle Charles' studio, Janine caught a glimpse on the easel of the painting he had been working on. This one was of Grandmother's summer kitchen in Les Fougères, framed within climbing roses. Uncle Charles was a painter of landscapes. He was also in the Resistance. And when he was not at the local theater, painting for theatrical groups coming from Paris to perform in La Rochelle, or downstairs, peeling apples for the dark-flour pies Aunt Marie baked on Fridays to sell in her grocery store on Saturdays, he painted. His paintings must have been successful for he had painted several lately. Once they were finished, he delivered them to whoever had ordered them. From her rooftop, Janine often saw him hurry out of the house, his beret down the side of his face, the finished painting under one arm.

Downstairs, Madeleine and Georges, Aunt Marie's employees, came into the dining room and were waiting at the basement door. They had put up and barred the store's wooden panels. With them was Mr. Khoeler. He was in the store when the alarm had sounded. Ever since the weather was cooler, he wore a long, gray cape. The hood bunched up behind his head made him look like a question mark. With no time for handshakes,

Uncle Charles and he acknowledged each other with a grunt. Aunt Marie came in from the kitchen, her cat, Ripus, following her. Frightened by the sirens, Ripus ran past everyone down to the basement as soon as Uncle Charles opened the door.

In preparation of alerts, Aunt Marie had set up two wooden benches between the steps and the coal allotted for her year's baking, heaped beneath the basement window.

Janine and Danielle huddled on a bench next to Aunt Marie. Madeleine and Georges sat on a bench across. Uncle Charles and Mr. Khoeler remained standing. Ripus had disappeared.

As soon as the sirens stopped wailing, a heavy silence settled as if the utterance of a single word were a beacon to the planes. Janine kept her teeth clenched to subdue their clattering as if this too could signal the planes over them. Next to her, Danielle, at times, shivered. Janine prayed silently that if the planes of the Royal Air Force came today, they would remain along the uninhabited part of the coast where, Uncle Charles had said, the Germans were already building a submarine base and bunkers, like barnacles along the shore. He had had fighting experiences in the trenches of Flanders during World War I. A piece of shrapnel remained lodged against the bone of one leg and hurt him whenever the weather changed.

Once, upon returning from the rooftop, Janine had walked into the kitchen when her aunt and uncle were there alone. He was talking as he shoveled coal from a bin into the big furnace. At the table, Aunt Marie was setting pies in rows of two on a huge spatula, which she used to slide them in and out of the oven. Their backs turned to Janine, they had not heard her come in.

" . . . so far, with their accent, they passed for Belgians. They have a Belgian passport," he said, pausing before refilling the shovel. Flames roared out of the open furnace. "But they are British and they have to return to England before the *Boches* catch on to them." He shoveled the coal in, and the flames, temporarily smothered, reappeared and settled around the coal. He closed the furnace door, leaned the shovel against the side and stood, one foot on the edge of the bin.

Her lower teeth grating against an ill-fitting bridge, her head bent, Aunt Marie increased and decreased, then increased and decreased again by the width of a nail the space between the pies. "What with the German land mines. . . . Be careful."

"The British leave from Spain. We help them into the free zone. Others over the Pyrenees. We also have a local network to smuggle the information I get. The *Boches'* big *Berthas* and anti-aircraft machinery must also be sabotaged before any Allies' raid."

That was how Janine had learned that Uncle Charles was in the Resistance, by happening upon a conversation which was not intended for her. Should she tiptoe back out? Just then, he turned around. He brought a finger to his lips. "*Motus,*" he said when he saw her. "Mum's the word!" he repeated.

"On my heart," Janine said.

Now, in the basement and from far away, the rumbling of a plane was heard. Her anxiety shot up like the mercury of Grandmother's outdoor thermometer in the August sun.

Uncle Charles exchanged a concerned glance with Mr. Khoeler. "They don't have enough information yet," he grumbled.

The throbbing of the motor became sharper. Grew. Rumbled overhead. Shoulders hunched, eyes riveted to the ceiling, they waited. Then Uncle Charles said, "It sounds like a reconnaissance plane." All eyes turned to him. "Probably German, scanning the sky for planes. There's no fire exchange."

And tension lifted like the morning mist.

The plane rumbled over La Rochelle for a long time, then droned away. Even though nothing could be heard except for the occasional whistle of the *défense passive* volunteer probably sending a premature passerby back to a shelter, the end of the alert did not sound. Aunt Marie heaved a sigh of relief.

"Had you set the *brioches* to rise?" she asked Georges.

"I was about to when I heard the sirens. So I helped Madeleine put up the store shutters instead."

"The howling startled me," she said.

Janine got up, glanced up at Uncle Charles, went to stand next to him. Everyone would continue telling what he was doing when the sirens sounded and her moment of reckoning for her rooftop meandering would come.

Sure enough, Aunt Marie asked. "Where were you, girls?"

"In the attic," Danielle said.

"I . . . was on the roof," Janine said.

"On the roof! What on earth were you doing there?"

Janine looked down at her feet. She did not answer.

"Don't you know you could. . . ."

"She's all right," Uncle Charles intervened as if he knew why ten-year-old girls walked on rooftops. He tousled the top of Janine's short hair.

"Promise you won't do that again," Aunt Marie said.

Janine did not want to promise. She kept staring at the ground.

"She'll be all right," Uncle Charles said.

She returned to her seat.

His gray coat encircling him like a moat around a fortress, Mr. Khoeler listened, as intimidating as he must have been in his classroom. He began talking with Uncle Charles about how the French had been betrayed by Marshal Pétain last spring and how they were now betrayed by the Vichy Government, who collaborated with the Germans. Each time Mr. Khoeler came to visit her uncle, their conversations returned to the same subject, and their voices rose and rose as if their angry pitch could still undo last May's debacle. As Uncle Charles talked and became angrier, he pulled his beret farther down his cheek. He brought it farther down now. Mr. Khoeler flung his cape about himself.

Even though he had been born in Alsace when it was still under German rule, before the 1918 Armistice returning it to France, he had always considered himself French, so he had told Uncle Charles. A widower, he lived alone in the apartment building next door and taught school in the non-occupied part of Bonvent, across the street from his apartment. He and Uncle Charles seemed to agree about everything they discussed and Janine often wondered whether he too was in the Resistance. His classroom was in the same building as a branch of the German *Kommandantur*.

"Listen," Aunt Marie said, placing her hand on Uncle Charles' arm. The humming of a motor, smoother than the choppy throbbing of the earlier plane, was clearly audible. Janine held her breath. So did everyone in the basement as tension again shot up. The Americans had the reputation of having smooth-sounding planes. Perhaps the Free French Forces or the British were using them? The humming increased until it was in the midst of them—in the loud purring of Aunt Marie's cat come out of hiding, now going from leg to leg, rejoicing in the reunion of so many friends in the same narrow spot.

The mono-sound of the all-clear resounded.

Everyone returned to his chores. Mr. Khoeler left.

Danielle and Janine had completed their homework the evening before. They were settling to read side by side at the dining-room table, but Aunt Marie needed the table to sort and paste food coupons with Madeleine.

"Now would be a good time for the girls' drawing lesson," Aunt Marie told Uncle Charles as he was about to return upstairs to his studio. He taught Danielle and

Janine on Thursdays, whenever he could not avoid it. He stopped short of the door to the stairway.

"Come on," he mumbled, his head motioning to come. Danielle closed her book and got up.

"May I bring my book and read instead?" Janine suggested as she got up. Unlike Danielle who had inherited her father's artistic talent, she was not good at drawing.

"When the hour is up," Uncle Charles said.

She followed her cousin and her uncle reluctantly. Not even her mother could guide Janine's clumsy hand.

In his studio, Uncle Charles with a sweep of his arm moved the objects from one half of the table to the other to make room for Danielle and Janine: the cans used as paint brush holders, the empty cigar boxes filled with pencils and drawing charcoals, the shoe boxes with half-empty tubes of paint. He picked up portfolios belonging to the rare private students—two or three, no more—whom he accepted to teach, provided they showed talent and the willingness to learn how to draw before they went on to painting, and placed them on a divan bed.

Danielle and Janine sat down at the table, their backs to the mantel where two recent paintings were drying. A couple more, waiting to be altered or delivered, leaned against the pulled down apron of the fire place. Others lined the divan bed against the wall.

Uncle Charles handed Janine a sheet of paper and a charcoal pencil. "Now draw lightly," he told her. "And don't overuse these." He passed the erasers out.

On a shelf across from the table, he placed a Grecian vase with frescos and a slender maiden in-between, offering food to a stylized cat-like animal. One eye closed, one arm stretched out, his thumb up, he moved it to follow from a distance the lines of the vase, explaining how to measure and draw the different parts of the vase proportionally to the whole.

"Now you draw," he told them. He slipped on his gray knee-length smock hanging behind the door, pushed his beret toward the back of his head, and went on to work on the current painting on the easel.

With a sure hand, Danielle was already sketching the outline of the vase. Then she busied herself with smoothing the neck opening. Janine too drew. But one side of the vase was as drawn-in as the cheeks of refugees she had seen come in from the east, while the other side protruded like the stomach of an expectant mother. She spent more time erasing and retracing than drawing. She put her chin in her hand and stared at the worn-out paper with overly accented lines, exactly what Uncle Charles had said not to do. She put her charcoal down and watched her uncle paint.

It was the climbing roses in many of his paintings that Janine found so striking. She watched as, out of thick red paint, he knife-carved roses against the green of foliage, all around Grandmother's summer kitchen door in Les Fougères, his easel set sideways from the window so that sidelight hit the background. Here and there, a rose stopped short of reaching the top of the door frame; others bent gracefully beneath, as if they were peeking inside the kitchen.

Uncle Charles was working on a rose stem. It grew under his paint brush and wove itself among and between others. Where would this one stop? She could not ask because when he worked—and he had been working overtime lately—he did not want to be disturbed. He stopped painting, searched the inside pocket of his jacket underneath the smock and took out a square of folded paper. He unfolded it. His head bent over it, he studied it carefully for a while. Holding it in one hand, he seemed to carve a rose with the knife he held in the other. He folded the paper, put it back in his inner coat pocket. He drew a stem more slowly than he had others, as if this one were the thread along which the rose at the end could always find its way. He brought the stem to a stop above the top right corner, among other red roses. After adding a touch of white gouache to the red on his pallet and blending the colors, he scooped a drop of the mixture and applied it to the rose at the end of the stem, making it a slightly lighter red.

He was finished. He poured kerosene on a swath of cloth, wiped the smeared paint off his pallet, cleaned his knife, and set his brush soaking in a jar with cleaning fluid.

"How's my Greek vase coming along?" he asked, wiping his hands off on his smock and coming over to Danielle to look at her painting.

Pleased enough by what he saw, he took the charcoal from her hand and showed her how to make the girl's gown appear more flowing. But when, over Janine's shoulders, he had taken one look at her drawing, he mumbled something she did not understand and took the eraser from her. As if in an afterthought, he tousled her hair.—Not everyone could be a painter. Then he looked at his watch, took his smock off, grabbed a painting on the divan bed, and bringing his beret back to the side of his face, walked out of the room almost as hurriedly as he walked out of Aunt Marie's store when a German was there.

There was not much he could have said, could he, about a vase which looked like a deflated bagpipe. Without haste, she put her drawing away inside a folder.

"I'm going to the attic," Janine said.

Danielle was perfecting the lines of the dress, as her father had said. She looked up from her paper. "Wait till I'm finished. I'll watch from the window. You know Mother. . . ."

"I'll be all right," Janine said, echoing Uncle Charles' words earlier.

She climbed the steps to the attic slowly. She did not want Uncle Charles to equate her with her drawings. But what if he did? As an adult, he could see things she could not. Wasn't he right about the war, about what ought to have been done, about what should be done now? No one, not even Aunt Marie, would question that. She had other areas of disagreement. Trusting Marshal Pétain, for instance, because he had been the hero of last war, whereas Uncle Charles and Mr. Khoeler called him a "sell-out" and a traitor.

Marshal Pétain, as vice-premier of France in the frantic days of last May, as Janine heard Uncle Charles and Mr. Khoeler discuss disconsolately again and again, had helped revise the French constitution so that France was no longer a republic now but a state—or, as her uncle put it, a dictatorship. Then in July, the Marshal had helped form a new government in collaboration with the Germans and, at 84, had become the chief of the new State of Vichy France. Aunt Marie believed that by talking with Hitler, Pétain was able to bring down the number of people shot each month by the German military in retaliation for opposing the occupation. Meanwhile, French people like Uncle Charles, and perhaps Mr. Khoeler, had answered General De Gaulle's June-the-eighteenth call from England to the French to continue their fight against the occupiers. Mr. Durand, a neighbor on the other side of the house, Janine had heard, was also in the Resistance. She saw him occasionally from the rooftop, coming home from work, or whenever he came to see Uncle Charles in his studio. She knew his wife better because she often came to the store to buy groceries or to chat with Aunt Marie. It was against the raised side-edge of their roof that Janine hung onto to walk to the chimney.

From the attic window, the inviting world of rooftops stretched before her, the forbidding monster-sirens invisible from here. Aunt Marie had said that Janine could get hurt. But then Aunt Marie had never walked on a roof herself. Not as Janine did, with her mother as her guide.

Janine clambered over the window sill and walked sideways along the narrow strip between the Durands' roof and the panes to Aunt Marie's chimney and paused. Atop the Bonvent School, the back to back sirens mouthed their silent threat.

They won't blare again today, will they? she asked her mother.

No, her mother said, it's enough for today.

When she reached Mr. Khoeler's roof, she crouched in the space between the crest and the skylight. Once, she had let herself slide from the skylight down to the landing below and had explored the stairway toward other floors, but only once, because at any moment he might surge out of his apartment, and a stern look on his face, ask her what she was doing here. And perhaps suggest to her aunt and uncle that she copy 'I shall not be a nosy girl' a hundred times.

Her chin resting on the crest of the roof, she watched––as if it were the stage of the *Guignol* at the Luxembourg Gardens where her mother took her occasionally when Janine was five and she and her parents still lived in Paris––part of rue Gambetta onto which Aunt Marie's store opened, the intersection between rue Gambetta and rue Thiers, and at the angle of the two streets, the Bonvent School with one of its facade on rue Thiers and the other on rue Gambetta.

It may have been close to noon. Mrs. Durand, her shopping bag bulging, returned home from the big market down the street. She hurried, probably for a last stop in Aunt Marie's store before it closed at precisely noon, per a newly enforced city ordnance.

Walking briskly, Uncle Charles appeared on rue Gambetta, coming back from the errand which had called him out of his studio earlier. He seemed early for the noon meal, which was never before one o'clock because Aunt Marie and Madeleine finished serving the customers who were already in the store before closing time. After crossing the intersection between the two streets, he disappeared from Janine's sight.

On rue Thiers, farther down, a German officer came out of the Bonvent building just as Uncle Charles returned, a painting under his arm. They both reached the corner of the school at the same time. As Uncle Charles kept up with his fast pace, the German drew back to let him pass before turning the corner behind him. Later, Mr. Khoeler who, now that the day was warmer, had traded his heavy cape for a lighter one, came within the intersection, heading in the same direction, toward the market place.

Janine stood up. It was time to go downstairs to help Danielle set the table. It's almost one o'clock. I must leave, *Maman.* But I'll be back soon, she promised her mother.

She made her way back carefully to the attic.

Downstairs, Danielle was already setting the table. Against the frosted glass separating the dining room from the store on this side of the room, Aunt Marie had pasted a large picture of Marshal Pétain. Janine read backward the words printed in large white letters beneath his white collar: *"Connaissez-vous mieux que lui les problèmes de l'heure?"*

She repeated the words out loud. "Do you know today's problems better than he?"

"Has Uncle Charles seen this poster?" she asked Danielle.

Danielle shook her head no and, raising her brows slightly, looked at Janine. "Mom and Madeleine just pasted it up. After Dad left."

"Oh," Janine said.

Helping Danielle set the table while Aunt Marie and Madeleine busied themselves in the kitchen, Janine brought the silverware out and set it on the table. A knock on the store door made her raise her head. Through the sheer curtain over the clear glass window between the dining room and the store on that side of the room, she saw Uncle Charles waiting for someone to let him in. She ran into the store and unlocked the outside door for him.

He swept past her. A rolled up newspaper under one arm, he walked to the poster, ripped it off the frosted glass. Crumpling it into a ball, he stormed across the dining room, into the kitchen, and hurtled the ball into the garbage can. "Turncoat! Traitor!" He brought his beret flat down one side of his face.

Aunt Marie stopped stirring the onions and potatoes for the meatless meal. Madeleine stopped tossing the salad. Her spatula above the frying pan, her teeth gnashing, Aunt Marie shook her head. "Why are you reacting so violently? The Germans shot one hundred men each week in Bordeaux until he took over. He brought an end to it."

"You call fifty stopping it? How long do you think before it's two hundred? Thousands?"

Aunt Marie raised her shoulders. "Charles!"

"Hundreds of thousands!" He was livid with rage. Aunt Marie did not answer. Somewhat calmer, he added. "Have you seen the paper?" He flipped it open before her.

She turned the flame down under the potatoes, handed the spatula to Madeleine who took over stirring them. Aunt Marie took the paper from him, stared at it. Her teeth grated faster.

Uncle Charles turned around—and around again—as if he wanted to escape from a cage. Stentorian, his voice shook with accusation. "He sold us out last May. He is selling us now!"

Motionless against a kitchen wall, Janine and Danielle watched. Georges ran in from the baking room where he had been mixing dough for Saturday's pies, and stood, immobile, in the doorway, his hands dripping with gray war-time flour.

Her clenched teeth grinding more slowly, Aunt Marie handed the paper back to Uncle Charles without a word. He held it up for everyone to see. The picture of Pétain shaking hands with Hitler covered the entire front page.

Silence settled as if the inner black-padded doors of a church had closed on them.

Aunt Marie stopped gritting her teeth altogether. Staring at the wall above Janine's and Danielle's heads, she seemed to be in a trance.

Convinced, perhaps, that the Marshal's betrayal and its consequences had sunk into her head, into everyone's head, Uncle Charles folded the paper accordion-like and thrust it next to the poster in the garbage can. He took a step to leave the room when Aunt Marie spoke. Her eyes locked into his, her voice pleaded: "He can't have been a hero in 1918 and be a traitor now."

His face ashen gray, as ashen gray as the smock he wore when he painted, Uncle Charles fled the kitchen. "Country of fools. House of fools."

His shoes hammered the steps to his studio.

He refused to come down for the meal, and Aunt Marie herself ate little. Normally striving to remain cheerful to cheer up those around her, she seemed stricken.

Sitting across from her at the table, Janine saw her lips move: "An unfortunate handshake. . . . But the situation was such. . . . He had to." Her eyes searched everyone for support. "To soften the situation, that is." Yet even she, did not seem convinced.

Soon she got up, went into the kitchen and returned with a plate of potatoes and salad. She took them upstairs. Was gone less than two minutes. Came back, the untouched plate in her hands.

While she was gone, Madeleine had brought a basket of apples from the kitchen and handed one to everyone for dessert. As she returned the basket to the kitchen, she bumped into Aunt Marie.

Aunt Marie brought the basket back. Absent-mindedly, she, too, began distributing apples. Realizing her mistake, she set the basket on the floor next to her chair. She sat down, her teeth grinding, silently grinding.

Janine slid her apple in her pocket. Her uncle would be hungry later in the afternoon. She would keep the apple for him.

Drying the dishes as Madeleine washed them and Danielle put them away seemed a more endless task than ever. Her pocket bulged with the apple, and each time she raised her hand to set a dried dish on the table, her wrist bumped against it. At last, the last dish was put away.

"I'm going to practice my cross stitch," Danielle said.

Janine also had to practice for her sewing class, but first she wanted to take the apple to her uncle. And go to the attic. She had promised her mother.

"I'll join you later," she said.

Uncle Charles' door was closed. She knocked lightly, heard a grumble which might have been "come in" as well as "keep out," and went in.

His beret still hiding the side of his face, bending over the table next to a finished painting of Grandmother's garden, he measured distances between several points on what seemed to be a hand-drawn map. Then pushing the paper aside, he made light pencil marks on the painting, among Grandmother's roses. He reached for the paper again and once more measured the distances slowly. Satisfied, he took the painting off the table, and placed—slammed it almost—on the easel.

He now rifled through a shoe box on the table and snatched a pencil out. He aimed it at a spot on the painting as if it had been the Marshal's head. He did not look at Janine, unaware of her presence, so absorbed was he.

She tiptoed to the table, took the apple out of her pocket, placed it next to the sketch Uncle Charles had used. In his haste, he had not bothered to put it away. It was a crude drawing of the coast. A few wavy lines for the ocean here. A sinuous curve for the shoreline there. The rectangle formed by Grandmother's kitchen door enclosed a portion of land and sea. Along the sides of the door and at intersecting lines within, small crosses crisscrossed the area like birds in flight. She tiptoed back out, closed the door softly behind herself.

"Don't slide off that roof, now," Uncle Charles gruff-sounding voice warned from behind the closed door.

That evening, the sewing session over, Danielle and Janine once again sat at the dining-room table, going over their oral assignments for the next day in case they were called upon to answer questions in class.

Through the sheer curtain over the window separating the store from the dining-room, Janine watched Aunt Marie and Madeleine busy themselves with the last-hour customers crowding in the store before curfew. A German officer came in and stood in line. Janine startled and stiffened. He looked like the officer who had followed Uncle Charles this morning, as she had witnessed from the rooftop. Served customers peeled off one by one. New ones came in. When the officer's turn came up, he obligingly motioned for those behind him to be served first. And to show that he could wait, he stepped aside of the line.

Uncle Charles' shoes came clacking down the stairs. In the next instant, the door from the stairwell opened and the radio was flipped on.

Pom pom pom po-o-om. Pom pom pom po-o-om. The twice repeated three short notes followed by a long one from Beethoven's Fifth Symphony rolled the Morse-coded V through the room, announcing the BBC news broadcast.

Uncle Charles sat down at his place, turning sideways to place one ear against the radio on a shelf level with his shoulder. Crackling with static, a voice rose, alternatively audible and inaudible between crackles. Uncle Charles raised the volume.

"A German's in the store. He followed you this morning," Janine warned.

Just then, the dining-room door to the store opened and closed. Aunt Marie came in like a whirlwind. "A German is in the store," she whispered. And as Uncle Charles lowered the volume, keeping his ear against the speaker, she continued on her way to and through the kitchen, probably to the storage room because she returned carrying a large, unopened bag of beans. It was a pretense only, Janine was sure, that the supply of beans in the store needed refilling.

The static on the radio blurred the voices completely. Uncle Charles turned the volume back up.

The German walked closer to the dining-room door, leaned against the ice box on the other side of the window, waiting for Aunt Marie or Madeleine, whoever would finish first with other customers, to wait on him.

Worried, Janine twisted on her chair. She looked at Danielle who seemed just as concerned. "*Papa,* shut the radio off," she urged her father. He turned it down.

Just then the door opened and closed again on Aunt Marie.

"Really, Charles!" She sounded anguished.

He looked at her, at Danielle and at Janine, glanced into the store, and turned the radio down.

Aunt Marie reached over, shut it off and, straightening up, brushed a kiss on his forehead. She rushed back to the store.

Uncle Charles stood up. The room seemed too small for his pacing.

The next afternoon, when Janine came home from school about four fifteen, the German, the same one as last evening, was in the store, the only customer there. Standing as he had yesterday, between the counter and the ice-box, his back against it, he blocked the passage to the dining-room door, and since he was already speaking when Janine entered the store, speaking a perfect French, startled, she put her school satchel down in the middle of the floor and waited for him to let her go through. Behind the counter, Aunt Marie was also waiting until he had finished speaking to count and give him the change she held in her hand.

". . . and we, in Austria, do not like Hitler either," the German was saying.

Janine felt her eyes open wider as she looked at him then at Aunt Marie. It seemed unlikely that Aunt Marie would have said anything against Hitler herself, what with last year's posters warning: "The enemy seeks your confidence," or this year's more subtle but as unequivocal ones: "Words are made of silver, but silence is made of gold." For now, she said nothing, but her eyes blinking quickly in Janine's direction cautioned silence.

"Ah!" the German went on. "We, in Austria are under the Nazis' boot as much as the French. We don't like Hitler's regime, but there's nothing we can do. I was an officer in the Austrian army. From one day to the next, I was integrated into the German army. Any overt rebellion would have been crushed by Hitler's men." His voice rose slightly at the end of his statement, not so much as if he were asking a question as inviting a comment, an endorsement from Aunt Marie perhaps.

Janine looked at the officer's feet. From near knee-high black boots stopping where uniform knickers began, to wide belt over well-adjusted green-gray jacket with a bird of prey insignia above the pocket, to neat collar showing perhaps whatever rank his was, all the way to his officer's cap sporting the same insignia as his jacket and rising like a stop sign above the visor, he looked as German as the soldiers whose goose steps now and then clanked their warning to the population down rue Gambetta, as she often saw and heard from the rooftop. A little shorter, perhaps. Older, yes. With the trace of a paunch beneath the flaring jacket, he might have been forty.

"Are you from Vienna?" Aunt Marie asked as she placed the change in a tray and slid it toward him.

"Salzburg. Like Mozart. Austrians are musicians. And artists. Not soldiers."

Aunt Marie's teeth ground against each others. Perhaps. Perhaps.

As she let the conversation drop, the officer acknowledged Janine. "Your daughter?" he asked.

"My niece," Aunt Marie said. "Her father, my brother, lives in *zone libre*. Her mother passed away. Janine is to us like our own daughter Danielle until she can be reunited with her father.

"Ah, war is a terrible thing," the officer said. He turned toward Janine. "Learning German at school?"

"English," Janine said.

The officer went on making small talk. He had not picked up the change Aunt Marie had placed before him, as if he were lingering, waiting.

Behind Aunt Marie, the door to the dining-room opened under a firm push, and Uncle Charles, carrying a painting under one arm, stepped briskly into the store, his body forward, ready to forge ahead. He stopped short as if, instead of the officer's marked inclination of the head to salute him, he had come upon a barricade. The two men's eyes met briefly, then once again the German stepped aside to let him go through. But as Uncle Charles passed between the counter and the ice-box, "Ah, Monsieur Brienne is an artist," the German said. He extended both hands toward the painting. There was nothing Uncle Charles could do but let him look at it.

Holding the painting at arms' length, his back now to Uncle Charles, the officer turned so that the light set off the almost three-dimensional quality of the painting, nodding while, Janine thought, his fingers moved lightly against the edges as if making sure that it concealed no double back.

"I took art in Milan myself," he said in his confidential tone, which rose slightly into a question and invited a reply. As Uncle Charles said nothing, he added, "Appreciation mostly."

"My husband studied in Florence," Aunt Marie said, obviously to break the silence. It was becoming awkward. The back of her hand nudged Uncle Charles' elbow.

"Two years during the twenties." He tilted his large beret closer to his cheek. "*La Scuola di Belle Arti.*"

A smile flickered on the officer's lips before he turned toward Uncle Charles and handed the painting back to him.

"Ah, very nice," he said. "The real thing."

That early dawn, two days later, before night had released its grip over light, they came. A far away rumble, which might have been approaching planes, except that the sirens above the Bonvent School remained silent. Janine and Danielle sat up at once in the bed they shared. Listened. Pale strips of light underlined the closed shutters. The rumble grew like approaching gunfire, exploded into a burst of motorcycles, a din of jinns swarming through rue Thiers, filling the streets around the block, stopping in rue Gambetta before Aunt Marie's store.

And through heightened awareness, Janine knew that in each house ghostly figures in pajamas and nightgowns gathered for reassurance, as she and Danielle had gathered around Uncle Charles and Aunt Marie. And in each house, she knew, a braver hand behind closed shutters mustered up enough courage to part them a slit, enough to glimpse within eiderdown-thick mist blurred outlines of helmet clusters. And, as noiselessly as he had opened them, Uncle Charles drew the shutters closed again in his and Aunt Marie's bedroom, slipped on trousers and jacket over his pajamas, and reached for his shoes.

In the street below, the motorcycles were turned off as soon as they came to a stop, but with more coming, the roaring went on. A whistle blew. Then another. A harsh German order, and all the motors stopped at once. An ominous silence followed. Lasting. An eternity lasting.

"Charles, *le grenier*," Aunt Marie said. "Quick, the attic."

There, opposite from the bay window, where the ceiling slanted toward the floor but for a one-meter high space, a man could lie flat as if within a coffin, behind a false wall made of sliding plaster boards.

"No," Uncle Charles said. "They know I'm here. If they didn't find me, they'd come after you." Moving past everyone, he flew upstairs toward his study, Aunt Marie behind him, repeating like a litany, "The attic, Charles! Charles, the attic."

Another German order ripped the silence. Immediately after, an angry, incessant fist pounded on what sounded like the store shutters, or perhaps the Durand's door.

"*Papa! Papa!*" Danielle cried running upstairs after her father.

Janine followed her, joined her hands into a prayer. "*Maman!* Please, ask God to help Uncle Charles!" God had not heard Janine when, last summer, by Grandmother's summer kitchen in Les Fougères, she had long prayed under the rain for her mother to live. But perhaps he would hear her mother, now close to Him.

Downstairs fists continued pounding. Angry, accented voices called, "*Ouvrez!*" Then whistles. Then more pounding. Then in German what may have been open up.

Janine reached the next landing as Uncle Charles came out of his studio, inserting the paper he had used as a map in an already stuffed envelope.

He handed it to Aunt Marie, "In the attic. Behind the wall." He had left the painting on the easel. He motioned toward it. "To Khoeler today."

Gritting her teeth, Aunt Marie nodded yes.

The time of a brief embrace—Aunt Marie then Danielle. With no time left, he tousled Janine's hair as he swept past her on his way down, his heels stabbing the steps in answer to the voices, the whistles, the increased pounding outside.

Aunt Marie hurried upstairs, her robe, which, in her distress, she had forgotten to tie over her long cotton nightgown, swishing and dusting behind her from wall edges to banister posts.

Tears streamed down Danielle's cheeks. Her hand cupped over her mouth, she had turned into a statue. Janine took her arm in her hand. "Come with me," she said. Danielle followed her downstairs to the dining room.

Suddenly, the pounding on the store shutters grew silent. The thud of men throwing their weight against the Durands' door replaced it. The door cracked. The pounding on the store resumed.

Holding on to each other and trembling, Danielle and Janine watched Uncle Charles from behind the sheer curtain on the window as he removed the indoor steel bar from across the store shutters, the angry fist behind now waiting. But it was from next door, from the Durands' house that they heard the final snap of a door caving in.

The shutters down, Uncle Charles unlocked the door and opened it. He took a step toward the Durands.' A cordon of men stepped forward, forced him back into the store. Three German SS, the double threat of their black skull insignia above the top pocket of their uniforms, walked in. They ordered him back into the dining-room then behind the table with Danielle and Janine.

"*Non! Non!*" The muffled sound of a woman's scream came in through the wall.

"Search," one of the SS told Uncle Charles. In no time, the drawers in the dining-room were ransacked, their content spilled onto chairs, table, floor. Two of the SS headed toward the kitchen, the baking and storage rooms while, across the table from the group, pacing the length of the room, one SS, the leader probably, guarded them.

Mrs. Durand's voice, so shrill and at other times so choked with anguish that it was unrecognizable, pierced through a jumble of angry commands, pounding boots, blows, coming through to them despite the thick adjoining wall.

In the dining-room, his hands behind his back, the SS kept on pacing.

Aunt Marie had not yet returned from the attic, and already the other two SS were returning from searching the baking areas.

And Janine looked at Danielle, her face as white above her robe as pre-war flour. "Mother," she read on Danielle's lips.

"Aunt Marie," Janine's lips formed for Danielle because the SS were going toward the door to the staircase.

Despite the one SS pacing along the length of the table, Uncle Charles, his blood drained from his face, his eyes set and shining as if he had a fever, lunged past the table toward the door.

Two clicks of his boots, and the Gestapo agent barred his way. Uncle Charles side-stepped him. Another click, and again the SS barred his way. Janine held her breath. She had heard of family men being shot on the spot for trying to defend their family. The papers had warned that such was the price for resisting any action undertaken by the occupiers. But no sooner had the other two SS turned into the staircase that they stepped back into the dining-room. Aunt Marie carrying her cat appeared in the doorway. The two SS exchanged a glance. The SS barring Uncle Charles' way had turned to see what was happening. With an imperious gesture, he ordered Uncle Charles and Aunt Marie behind the table.

And Janine saw that blood was flowing again in Uncle Charles and Danielle's faces and felt it running through her own. Aunt Marie put the cat down. He disappeared into the kitchen.

The sound of struggles still filtered through the walls.

From above, doors banging, moved furniture scraping floors, steps groaning, told them where, now, the search upstairs was taking place.

As if coming from another dimension, a truck shrouded in the morning fog rumbled in the street. Janine saw it stop before the store.

The two SS returned from their search upstairs, their arms loaded with several of Uncle Charles' paintings. They dumped them onto the table for the leader to see. He held one, looked at it, and raising it above his head after feeling the wood backing, he brought the painting down on his knee and broke it in half; he examined one piece, twisted it and tried to part it, probably in case thin layers of wood glued together concealed papers or photographs in-between. Finding none, he went through the same ritual with other paintings, dumping them on the floor when he was through. Laughing as he made a remark in German, he pointed at all the painted roses. The other two SS joined in the laughter. He gave the order to leave.

As they opened the store door, screams and protests, from the street this time, swept into the house, louder. Along the curb, the truck waited, the rear access gaping.

One SS on either side, holding him under the arms, Mr. Durand, his back arched to resist, was being dragged and pushed toward the truck bed. He freed one arm, reached back toward Mrs. Durand. She grabbed it, hung on to it. Soldiers tore her away from him. The two SS holding him took a step backward, then as if with uncoiling strength, hoisted him into the truck. The canvas fell over Mr. Durand.

Whistles blew and engines roared. A web of motorcycles, the truck in the center, swarmed away in a rumble as deafening as when the evil had first come. The roar decreased into a far away droning. The silence of a tomb settled in.

Aunt Marie, Uncle Charles and Danielle, hanging on to her father's jacket, ran to Mrs. Durand. Janine could not speak, could not cry. Dazed, she went up to her room, continued on toward the attic, the relief that Uncle Charles had not been taken away by the Gestapo and the horror mingling, forming a hurtful knot in her throat and in her chest.

She stopped at her uncle's studio. It had been ransacked. The tubes of paint, the pencils, and the charcoals out of their searched containers were scattered everywhere. The drawings of Uncle Charles' students, Danielle's, her own had been dumped on the divan bed, portfolios and folders thrown on the floor. Two paintings on canvas were slashed. The Grecian vase had rolled under the table in one piece but cracked. The chimney apron had been raised, the scattered ashes, searched. The easel stood empty, but beneath lay a bent yet unbroken painting.

She picked it up, examined it. She recognized at once the lighter red rose stopping above the frame of Grandmother's summer kitchen door. It was the painting that Uncle Charles had worked on during the last drawing session and that, he had said, should be passed on to Mr. Khoeler.

From behind the lace curtains on the window, she glanced in the street. Downstairs, past Aunt Marie's store, a German soldier, his rifle across his chest, marched up the sidewalk. Across the street, another marched down. They might patrol the street all day, and Uncle Charles would never be able to leave with a twisted painting under his arm, or with any painting at all. When, earlier this morning, he had told Aunt Marie, "To Khoeler, today," it sounded urgent.

Holding on tight to the painting, Janine climbed the last flight of stairs to the attic.

By the window, she set the painting against the wall. Should she? She looked outside. The roof and the chimneys wrapped in fog looked like a graveyard. She opened the window, leaned out cautiously in case German soldiers were mounting guard on rooftops. She could see none.

Maman, help me, she whispered.

She climbed over the window sill onto the roof, reached back inside for the painting.

Holding it flat against her along the narrow strip, her back to the Durand's wall, the panes stretching before her like a fogged-up pond, she made her way sideways to the chimney across, trusting her mother to steady her steps.

The morning dampness sipped through her robe. Her teeth clattered.

She had never talked to Mr. Khoeler. Wrapped in his cape, he was too intimidating. What would he say now upon seeing her? What would she say to him? Besides, what time was it? Would he have already left for school by the time she got to his door? And what if someone was with him? Someone like a German officer or an SS soldier inquiring about *his* activities? Her heart pounded faster. She leaned against the chimney. She heard her mother's voice within herself. Think, my Janine. Think.

To get a sense of time, she listened for the strangled horn of a rare car about to reach the intersection—none was supposed to circulate before seven—for schoolboys calling to each others on their way to school. But it seemed that only sirens could now break the stillness.

Belying her thought, a rhythmic pounding broke through, the goose steps of a German patrol farther in the rue Gambetta. She crouched by the chimney, the painting flat on the roof next to her. The boots hammered their warning past Aunt Marie's store.

The patrol, when it came, came early. Mr. Khoeler would be home.

Again, she imagined her mother's voice. It cautioned, Be careful.

Maman, help me.

How will you be sure that Mr. Khoeler is home alone?

By knocking on his door?

With the painting?

I'll check first without it.

Where will you leave it?

Right here, behind the chimney?

What if someone should look out the skylight?
Wouldn't they see it?

Isn't it too early. . . . Unless the couple on the first
floor. . . . Who is the couple on the first floor?

Be brave, my Janine.

After the patrol had passed, she picked the painting
up, went back a few steps and set it next to the Durands'
wall where it could not be seen from a distance. The fog
was thinner. To avoid being seen, she crawled. Down
the slant of one roof. Up the side of the other. At last
the skylight. As when she had first explored beneath, it
was closed but unlatched. She raised the dome, insert-
ed her hand inside, and found the crank. She turned it
until the skylight was wide open. Her hands gripping
the edge of the roof, she dropped down as lightly as she
could onto the landing, less than a man's height below.
She stood still, listening, in case someone had heard
her. She had just gone down a few of the steps separating her from Mr. Khoeler's floor when he appeared on
his doorstep. Fully dressed for school in a dark gray
smock belted at the waist over dark trousers, he looked
as forbidding as in his cape. A look of surprise crossed
his face. She froze, her eyes level with his.

"I came. . . . My uncle said. . . . To bring you roses."
It was not what she had meant to say. "He said today.
You must have them today."

"The painting!" he said, reaching for his cape. He
glanced up and down the staircase.

Just then, he brought a finger to his lips, motioned
for her to hurry inside the apartment and closed the
door behind himself. From the floor below came the

sound of bolts being drawn, of a door opening and closing, of the brisk turning of a key. Light footsteps followed by heavier ones hurried down the steps, along the hallway, outside.

Janine looked at Mr. Khoeler. "Spies?" she asked, her fear of him forgotten.

"A couple on their way to work. The least others know, the better." He added, "I'll go and get the painting."

"No," she said. "It's on the roof. I'll bring it to you. Guards are patrolling the streets."

He helped her through the skylight. "Be careful."

But she would be all right. How could he know that someone watched over her far more efficiently than all the guards with their guns strapped across their chests?

She walked down the side of Mr. Khoeler's roof. The Durands' chimney, a roof away from Uncle Charles and Aunt Marie's , looked like a marker.

Bend down, her mother reminded her.

At the Durands' wall, she retrieved the painting. Bending down again, her mother watching, she retraced her steps toward Mr. Khoeler waiting beneath the skylight.

She handed him the painting.

"You did a fine job," he said.

She nodded to acknowledge the compliment, with a silent thank you to her mother.

He added: "Tell your uncle same time, same place tomorrow."

Robert Barany

My experience with writing had been the usual relating to thirty-six years of teaching. This included writing goals and objectives, departmental directives, federal grants, accreditation reports as well as daily communications. Having retired, and my wife being a member of this workshop, I decided to join and perhaps expand my writing experience to include a few memoirs.

"A Widow's Validation" deals with an experience I had as a second grade student. I was challenged in front of my classmates to view a man lying in state. Embarrassed and not wanting to go, I felt compelled to accept this challenge so as not to appear weak in front of my peers. This acceptance led me to an experience I could not have imagined.

A Widow's Validation

Our four-room, two-story brick school house was located on top of a hill overlooking the eastern outskirts of a small town in the foot-hills of the Appalachian Mountains. Each teacher taught two grades. The two rooms on the first floor, located near the entrance, were for the first- to fourth-grade students. The two rooms on the second floor were for the sixth- to eighth-grade students. The principal taught the seventh and eighth grade in the room nearest the office.

All the second grade students were in their class-room, forming a line for dismissal at the end of the school day. My friend Jim was already in front of the line, which was near the door, while I was only half-way across the room. Our teacher was standing outside the door in the hallway talking with a fellow teacher, while we were eager to form our dismissal line.

"Hey, Bob. Bobby!" Jim said to me in a rather loud voice from the front of the line.

"What do you want?" I asked with some reserva-tion. Jim was always trying to do something new or different. Most of my classmates and I were happy to just follow rules and try to be successful with the usual daily activities.

"Wanna see a dead man?" Jim asked. I was stunned. I stopped walking and did not offer an immediate reply.

Jim had a smile and broke the silence he had antici-pated with a loud and demanding, "Well?"

"Well what?" I said, irritated while looking at the other students whose eyes were turning toward me.

Jim repeated his question in an exaggerated tone of exasperation. While moving his head from side to side to emphasize each word, he said, "Do-you-want-to-see-a-dead-man?" He had a way of making his thoughts known, and using his head as a metronome was one way to try to get everyone in the classroom to watch, hear and grasp the impact of his question.

Most of the other students became quieter, some smiling and many looking to see my reaction. I had just been invited to commit a possible social taboo and, because I was a boy, some expected me to do this sort of thing. Jim could have asked me earlier in the day, when we were alone, but he waited for this time to make this challenging invitation in front of all my classmates.

With the most confident smile I could show, I replied, "Yea, sure." I wished my voice had been louder.

Jim quickly answered with a prepared comment. "Okay. I'll meet you outside on the front steps after we're dismissed."

"See you then." I said, trying to be quicker with my response. The decision was made. This ordinary day filled with predictable events suddenly turned into a benchmark day. A day to remember. Forever.

The dismissal line was formed with Jim in front waiting with a smile. He always seemed to be at the lead, even in this line so carefully organized and designed by our teacher. This line system offered teacher control of all the students until we were dismissed by the teacher and not by the dismissal bell set to go off by the clock.

The large clock on the wall appeared to be somewhat broken. I never realized how slowly the pendulum moved back and forth. Finally the bell rang, but our teacher did not dismiss us. We stood silently and my anxieties grew, eager as I was to start my new adventure. We heard other classes leaving and we were still standing, good, silent and resentful. Our teacher slowly walked along the side of our line, searching for an excuse to keep us under her control. The last lesson of the school day was not the bell but our teacher, and only our teacher, could dismiss us.

Our dismissal was preceded by the usual warning from her. "Do not run through the hall and out the door," she said. This warning was followed by her daily reminder, "You are young ladies and gentlemen and do not run in a building." We left quietly and orderly for fear she would call us back into the room. She had that kind of power.

I went to the front of the school and saw Jim on the steps waiting for me as he had promised. Ed, another classmate, was also waiting with Jim and was asking if he could come along. After much hesitancy and pretense of thought, Jim agreed to allow Ed to join us. Jim's permission was granted only if Ed promised to follow his lead. Jim explained that when we would get to the house, he would go first, I would be next, and then Ed was to follow me. We were to do everything exactly as Jim would say and do. Ed and I agreed to this plan and were ready to get started. Maybe Jim had learned people control from our teacher.

The other children were running down the walkway and down the hill as if to get to a more desirable place as soon as possible. At the end of the school day, most of the children followed the sidewalk, which zig-zagged, down the steep hill. They had to take a few steps down to a declining walkway that led eastward, then a few steps down to a declining walkway that led westward. This progression was repeated until it reached the bottom of the hill. The paved walkway was also outlined with rails made of metal pipes. The railings were there to help keep the children on the sidewalk and were essential in winter to offer some assistance in helping them down the hill when there was snow and ice.

There was also another route down the hill which was taken by some of the more daring students when there was no snow, ice or mud. A dirt path, offering a much shorter and faster route, led straight down the hill. The children who chose this steep path were sliding, slipping, running with arms waving to help keep their balance and always laughing.

At the bottom of the hill where the sidewalk and dirt path ended, were two eighth-grade boys with shiny badges pinned on a wide belt that wrapped around their waist and criss-crossed their chest. They also held a long bamboo pole with a red flag at the end with the word STOP printed with large white letters. These flags were made by PTA volunteers. This was the School Patrol and no one would cross the street to get to the sidewalk which led through the town and to their homes without the older boys using their poles with flags to stop oncoming cars.

As we started down the hill, Jim added, "I've already seen him two times." It felt good to be led by an experienced person.

Jim avoided the front of the house, which had a dark wreath on the door, and led us to the back porch. He whispered that they didn't want people entering through the front door so as not to disturb the dead man and the mourners. We would not have known that if Jim wasn't our leader. He opened the back door slowly and quietly, leading us directly into the kitchen. We proceeded slowly and tried to be as solemn as possible while carrying our books, art work, and empty lunch pails.

Forming a short line of three-second grade students, we stopped when Jim pointed to a large book on a metal stand and whispered that we were to sign our names. I didn't know I would have to do anything like that. What if my parents found out what I was doing? The book had been placed on a stand too tall to allow us easy access. Ed and I looked at Jim for a solution when a woman, the widow, brought the book down from the stand and held it for us to sign. After Jim signed, it was my turn. I quickly changed my lunch pail from my right hand to my left hand, which caused the pail to hit the stand. The sound of metal hitting metal caused a disturbance sufficient to stop all talking. A man gave me a stern look, but the widow kept her smile. I was so nervous while signing my name, I was almost happy that it looked so scribbled. Maybe no one could read it and my parents would never know. After the signing, the widow carefully returned the book to the stand while continually smiling. She seemed so happy we were here that it puzzled me.

We proceeded into the front room, where the casket, surrounded by flowers, was located next to the wall at the left of the front door. Grown-up people, all dressed in black, were seated along the opposite wall, watching us, the newcomers. My bright red sweater made me feel uncomfortable. Jim never said anything about having to wear black.

Jim slowly walked toward the casket. I followed and Ed trailed behind me. After a quick look at the deceased, this was his third time, Jim moved forward to allow me a turn. I quickly glanced at the man. I tried to see if he was breathing by looking at his chest. His chest was not moving. Looking at his face, I was surprised to recognize Harry who was always on the front porch when we went by after school. I stooped over for a closer look to make sure I was not making a mistake. I heard a woman ask, "What is that kid doing?" I quickly stood straight causing my lunch pail to hit the metal trim on the casket. The same metal-to-metal sound resonated throughout the room. All talking stopped and a man said, "It's that kid with the lunch pail again." I looked down and even seeing the picture of Superman leaping from a tall building that decorated the offending lunch pail did not give me comfort. A woman said, "They shouldn't allow children in here at a time like this." Red faced, I said nothing and moved forward. To move away from Harry and the casket gave me some sense of relief. Jim appeared as if on the verge of laughing. I appreciated his effort and sort of liked him better for not adding to my embarrassment.

It was now Ed's turn to see a dead man. I wondered if he was happy that Jim allowed him to come and what he thought about the dead man being Harry. Jim never said our first dead man was going to be Harry. Jim did things like that.

The kind widow was talking to the couple who had made the comments. I heard her say, "Isn't that nice. The children came to pay their last respects to Harry.

He always sat on the front porch to wave and talk with the children. He shared his love for fishing with them. Sometimes that was the most important thing in his day."

"Yes. We know." The woman said in a low voice. While looking at the floor, she added, "I just, well, thought Harry didn't care much for chil. . . ." Her voice trailed to a whisper after a nudge from the man seated next to her. The widow walked away from the couple after she added, "I just know Harry would have been pleased to know the children came to pay their last respects to him as their friend."

Ed finished his viewing and joined us, still looking solemn. The widow smiled, turned and thanked us again as we exited through the kitchen and out the back door.

I remembered Harry always sitting on his porch with his fishing gear, but he never waved or talked to us about fishing or anything else. We hardly knew anything about him other than his name. He was always asleep with his fishing gear next to him. One day we saw Harry remove a bottle from a basket that was part of his fishing gear, quickly take a drink, and return the bottle. We joked about old Harry being drunk again and after a while, we simply saw him as a porch fixture with fishing gear and not as a person.

As soon as we were outside and away from the house, Jim looked at me and asked, "Well, what do you think?"

Looking back at our leader, I responded, "You didn't tell us it was going to be Harry. I thought it was going to be a stranger or you would have said something. I was surprised it was Harry."

"Yeah, I thought you would be surprised," and ignoring my complaint, Jim said, "But what about his being dead?" He had made these arrangements for Ed and myself and wanted a reward in the form of some answers or at least some reactions.

Ed added that he was also surprised it was Harry but didn't care. This was also the first time he had seen a dead man and it didn't make any difference to him whether it was Harry or a stranger.

I felt outnumbered and compelled to make some kind of comment. With both Jim and Ed looking at me, I looked back and said thoughtfully, "Well, I don't know. Except for not breathing, he looked as if he was sleeping. The same as when he was on the porch. It doesn't seem to make a difference, but maybe, to Harry it does."

"Is that all?" Jim was obviously disappointed by my comments.

"Well, no." I added with some conviction. "I thought Harry's wife was strange. I thought a widow was supposed to be sad, and she smiled a lot around us. She seemed so pleased that we came, signed the book and all. In fact, she was especially pleased to tell the couple with the opinions about Harry's fishing story and how much he enjoyed our company."

I expected Jim to dismiss my comment, but he seemed uncomfortable and wanted to say something. "Bob, I think you have a point." He finally said. "That explains why, after my second visit, the widow gave me a quarter and said how nice it would be if more of my friends would come."

Coal Camp Entertainment

The general daily atmosphere in our coal camp was comprised of work, share, get along with everyone and survive. When entertainment took place, it was treated as a gift and appreciated by all. When the men got together to repair the road after winter weather, the women and children got involved and created a party atmosphere. This usually took place on a Saturday and ended in the evening when the sun set. By that time, the road would be repaired and our party in full swing.

I loved music but was not particularly fond of the music that was referred to as mountaineer or hillbilly music by my parents. My appreciation of this musical style certainly started when several of the young people would get together on a porch to play their guitars and sing. This was accepted as a home-grown concert offered on a cool summer evening. The breeze would carry the music through the camp, and most of the people would sit on their front porches to listen. The performers played by ear and had technique good enough to offer several variations with their songs. After several songs they offered a treat that I especially liked and never forgot. They would sing a song in close harmony, yodel for a while, and then finish with soft, harmonic tones as they carefully pronounced each word. I was so happy to live here and be able to hear what I considered music from heaven. Even though I pursued music later in life, I have yet to hear a group that could sing and play from the heart and yodel like those who were so generous with their talents and had lived in our unique coal camp.

Another memory of outstanding community entertainment was, at the age of six, being able to hear the great world heavyweight championship bout between the Brown Bomber, Joe Jouis, and James J. Braddock, who had defeated Max Baer in June 1935. Our neighbor, who lived across the street from our home, purchased a Philco floor-model radio, the first radio anyone owned in our company patch. This acquisition created a great interest, especially among the men. It was not unusual to see several men go in and out of our neighbor's home during an evening. Then, on June 06, 1937, our neighbor, with the help of several men, brought this piece of furniture out on his front lawn. It was in the evening and the men were moving quickly to attach an antenna, ground wire, electric cords and whatever it would take to get the radio to work in time for the boxing bout. They had great difficulty getting reception without static and kept trying every new idea that was presented. By this time, a small crowd of people, mostly from our end of the patch, had congregated on our neighbor's lawn. Everyone was talking and repeating the time as it got closer to the fight and the static was still dominant. One man left and soon came back with several bottles of homemade beer and a few jugs of moonshine. He claimed the moonshine may not help get rid of the static but it definitely would help with their hearing.

This uplifted the men's spirits. The women got together and decided to get some of their home-made bread and the neighbor, just above us, said she had several quarts of home-made apple butter. The children eagerly volunteered to help. It seemed like magic how everything got organized, and before long everyone was back with the treats. In the meantime, the men managed to cut the static down to an acceptable level.

The time came to hear the heavyweight championship bout of the world and I was sitting on our neighbor's front lawn with a piece of home-made bread covered with home-made apple butter feeling I was the luckiest boy in the world.

Mail-Order Bride, et al.

Mrs. DeBar had passed away prior to our moving on New Hill. Mr. DeBar and their son Wayne, who was in his late twenties or early thirties, continued to live together in the same house. Wayne was a single, very quiet man and was devoted to his father. His father was also named Wayne but was always referred to as Ole Man Debar. They were both coal miners and maintained a clean, neat house that lacked extra furniture or anything else that was not essential to their frugal and somewhat secluded way of life. They were considered honest, hard-working, dependable men who kept to themselves. They very seldom socialized with people living in the patch other than with their next-door neighbors. They retired earlier than most of the families, who devoted a lot of evening time cleaning the children and getting them ready for bed.

Ole Man DeBar owned a plow horse and was in great demand every summer when it was time for planting. Each house had access to a large backyard, approximately 80 X 40 feet, and every backyard got plowed. Even the men who did not want to be bothered with a garden planted one just to keep their wives from nagging them. The wives would make sure there were summer vegetables for their families and enough for canning in preparation for the winter months. Some of the men staked their tomatoes, hoed the corn, and carried water from a well, located on our end of the patch, to water the plants. Other gardens were neglected but somehow, miraculously, provided an abundance of vegetables. I remember seeing tomato plants which had not been staked, lying on the ground, heavy with large, red tomatoes. The West Virginia rains helped a lot and the "unwilling" gardeners depended on the rains to help bring success with the gardens and peace from their wives. The garden was a great source of food and was prized by the wives, especially during the coal mine strikes.

The various families would make arrangements with Ole Man Debar to plow their backyards. The willing husbands were always the first to get their yards plowed, followed by the unwilling husbands and their nagging wives. After a few years, a person knew who would get their yard plowed from the first to the last. The differences in the desire for plowing offered a schedule that allowed every yard to be ready for planting on time.

With the arrival of fall came the canning season and news that Ole Man DeBar was getting married to a "Mail-Order" bride. This news spread through the camp faster than a hound dog running after its first rabbit of the season and was received with a variety of reactions: "Well I'll be damned" or "You're joking." A few wondered what Wayne would think and some wondered what Wayne was thinking to let his dad commit such an unpredictable, unsettling act. I'm sure the wives were happy that planting season was over and were hoping the old man would come to his senses before the next year's planting season started.

There was a contrast in reaction between the men and their wives over this news. The wives considered it the DeBar debacle for the planting season as far as the community was concerned, and the men simply viewed it as a normal transition and failed to see any problems, especially the "unwilling gardener" husbands. There was no news about the wedding, which led to many discussions and predictions. This news blackout created and nurtured curiosity to a degree well above the norm. Anxiety was prevalent among the women to get this issue over.

The day finally came when we saw Wayne and his dad leave in their horse-drawn buggy to go to Worthington, which had a streetcar station and was the town nearest to New Hill. The bride was supposed to come from Arkansas by train to Fairmont, a city twenty miles away, and then to Worthington by streetcar. I joined the other children who were hiding in the bushes and behind small trees in an area that separated our dead-end road from the road that came from Worthington. This was the only road available and we wanted to be the first to see the new Mrs. DeBar, the "Mail-Order" bride.

To pass the time, we were pretending to be sword-fighting with branches from the small trees as swords when someone yelled, "They're coming." We dropped our swords and got to our hiding places to see the bride and groom. We had chosen places that would get us as close to the road as possible without being seen.

Our first view was a surprise when the horse and buggy came around the bend with the bride in charge of the horse. She was wearing a long, light-blue dress with small flowers imprinted in a scattered fashion. She also had on a matching bonnet. Ole Man DeBar was not smiling, and Wayne was riding in the back with some luggage. The woman appeared to be of the same age as the older DeBar and had a distinct feature. The bride had whiskers. We were so amazed that we almost jumped out of our hiding places for a closer look. We also noted the plow horse was moving faster than we had ever seen it move before. The buggy continued on the road that ran along the back side of the camp toward Hutchinson, a neighboring coal camp. This road also had a cut-off that allowed a vehicle to enter New Hill on the opposite end from where we lived.

We came out of the brush trying to express in words what we had seen. Everyone was talking fast and at the same time. The only let-up was when someone would start laughing, which was highly contagious, and the talking would stop for a while. As soon as we got on our road, a few women called us over to their porches to tell them what we had seen. They had more questions than we had answers but we tried to include everything. We knew we had important news when a woman told another to be quiet and let the kids talk. To be heard as well as seen was a rare and exhilarating experience. We told them about the horse's gait, who was driving, where Wayne was riding, the bride's whiskers and the expression on Ole Man Debar's face. This seemed to satisfy the women, who lost no time in getting the news to the other wives.

The DeBars did not arrive on New Hill as expected. They had continued their ride to Hutchinson and the chapel. The wives liked this part of the DeBar wedding story. When this event was later recalled during the evening conversations on someone's porch, they would tell how Hazel, the bride, took charge of the buggy, its destination and the sequence of events which included marriage before going to the DeBar house. This always met with the wives' approval and the men's disregard.

On the day of the bride's arrival, when the men got home from work, their wives shared this news of the day. Later in the evening, some men got together in small groups on different porches. The new marriage was discussed and some felt it was a bad omen for the DeBars. Not only did Ole Man DeBar not bring his bride home but she brought them back. The men took a "let's wait and see" attitude before coming to any definite conclusions. They did agree that this marriage, even with only a few strangers present as witnesses, was probably not as stressful as when the young couple, Jake and Susie, got married.

In contrast to the DeBar wedding, there were dozens of people at the home of the bride's parents celebrating the wedding of Susie and Jake. Most of the people were celebrating in the front yard and on the porch. Everyone was having a good time when four of Jake's friends grabbed him by the arms and legs and threw him over the porch banister into some rose bushes. Every time Jake tried to get up, he would moan when pricked by the thorns. This made his friends laugh even more. Jake took a deep breath, jumped up and out of the rose bushes. Anger was written all over his face as he stood and stared at his friends with his fists clenched. He turned around and started to run to his house. The laughter stopped when someone yelled, "Jake's going to get a gun!"

One of the four men who had thrown Jake over the banister said something like, "Jake never had and Jake never will have a sense of humor."

David, Jake's younger brother, ran after him, yelling, "Jake! Jake! Don't forget to load it." The four friends decided to catch up with Jake and talk to him. They left the celebration, as some other men joined them, to try to prevent Jake from doing something "foolish."

About an hour later, they all returned. They obviously had a little private party judging by the way some of them staggered. Jake was smiling and seemed friendly. He had changed his shirt that had been torn by the rose thorns and had his arm around Jim's shoulders. The story was told that Jim apologized to Jake but that Jake still wanted to get his pistol and eliminate their brand of humor. After much talk and appeasement, Jim offered to allow Jake to hit him so everything would be equal. Jim stuck his chin out for Jake, hoping Jake would pass on the offer. Jim offered again, stuck his chin out even more, closed his eyes, and told Jake to go ahead. Jake swung back and landed a punch in Jim's stomach. Jim went down moaning on the ground. It took a little while for him to get his breath. The other men helped him up, brushed him off and told him how nice Jake was not to have hit him in his face. All was forgiven for now, as they accepted Jake's threats to retaliate. Jake said he was going to grow a rose bed with the largest roses and longest thorns that he could find on the green face of this earth. He made them promise that they would jump in this rose bed at their own wedding celebration. They all promised, with some hesitation, and Jake exonerated Jim because he had just paid his debt. This was a gesture to ease Jim's pain and help get everything back to a friendly basis. They decided to drink to all of that and they returned to the group who had continued celebrating.

The fall weather continued and very quickly it was Halloween. One of the older kids introduced a new idea. He had heard about this from his cousin who lived in Ohio. It was called, "Trick or treat." The "Trick or Treat" approach to harassing neighbors on this special occasion was new to me. In the past, we would do things like knock on a door and run to hide. We would then watch to see if they would open the door, see no one, and make a comment like, "It's those damned kids again. I wish they would outlaw Halloween." We thought this was great fun, but this new "Trick or Treat" idea had some obvious benefits.

We went from house to house, surprising some people while others were ready for our begging threat, "Trick or Treat." Our onslaught spared no house. With reluctance, we knocked on the door of the new Mrs. DeBar, who was called Hazel by the wives, expecting to come face to face with the whiskered lady. The door opened and there she stood, "I've been expectin' you youngins'," she said. "Come on in," she added.

We had seen curtains from the outside, which was new for the DeBar house, and now we could see a table cloth on the table and even rugs on the floor. No doubt a woman now lived here and she was in charge. The biggest surprise was that she had no whiskers. Some women had made friends with her and her new appearance offered a surprise almost as pleasant as the plate of homemade cookies she was offering.

Ole Man DeBar even became more sociable. He actually joined the men on some of the gatherings that took place on a front porch in the evenings. The men told him, "You sure know how to pick 'em. She's a good wife. Knows how to cook like a whiz and keeps a clean house." The compliments were followed with a tease warning him to be careful. "She may take over your plowing business and kick you out." Ole Man Debar responded with, "Not a chance. She told me she's fallen in love with this old coal miner and our way of life. Wayne gets along real well with her and she cooks a lot of what Wayne likes. I'm a lucky man." No one argued with this summation and as usual, the group broke up for the evening for early retirement. Tomorrow was the start of another work day in the mines.

Bud Brower

After seven decades, while becoming jack-of-all-trades-master-of-few, I joined Ross's writing group to expand my horizons.

My wish to share experiences from America's greatest moments has progressed from latent desire to a series of written accounts meant to be shared with family and friends. Thanks to the group, my ramblings are rounding into blurbs of humorous observations, even a history-based novel. The group's encouragement tempts me to write beyond my mediocre poetry of the 1980s.

Nothing should be considered more American than the industry of oil. Disagree if you will, but think about it—the petroleum industry was born in America. The modern oil industry began in 1859 with the first well drilled and developed in western Pennsylvania. From that point on, the doors of opportunity opened to build a better quality of life for America and other developing nations far into the foreseeable future. Many in the world now condemn this industry, a great number of whom are Americans. Why this should be is puzzling.

Historically, America has led the world in commerce. Agriculture, transportation, chemistry, electronics, space age industry—all have benefited from petroleum's con-

tribution to earth's standard of living. In our lifetimes we've witnessed, and prospered in, the developing high-tech computer age—totally dependent on petroleum products. Ours and our children's futures will depend heavily on the continuing production of earth's petroleum resources far into the foreseeable future. At the very least, until a better source of energy is discovered to take its place, we will continue being dependent on it.

Morning Tour relates experiences from a working American family that overcame most of life's adversities. Commencing with the 1930s depression—building through our modern computer-generated times—it's a story paralleled by millions of America's citizens who can relate to the Davis family's success story. Going from rags to riches, the old fashioned way. The best part: America, with her educational and experimental abilities intact, remains the leader for our modern world while we continue to lengthen and improve the lives of its inhabitants.

I hope you enjoy the read as much as I enjoyed the writing.

Morning Tour [pronounced "tower"]

September 1983

Jake's eyes snap open with the first klaxon horn blast. Bare feet ignore the damp discomfort of cold steel decking. He scans his offshore drilling rig for signs of serious trouble. "This is Jake Davis!" he shouts into the phone. *"Is this a test?"* Then, impatiently, he waits for his answer.

"This is a test! Repeat, this is a test: 0537." A digitalized voice echoes through the superstructure, rasps in his ear. Turning, observing his minions scrambling to emergency stations during an early hour fire drill, a rare smile creases

Jake's weathered face. He enters the time, 0537, in the ledger.

"Making pretty good moves for an old man, Jake," a lanky derrick hand, moving toward the galley and a rock-ribbed breakfast, is needling him.

"It's your ass the day I don't," Jake mumbles. His aging body shakes as cold steel decking registers its presence. "Morning tour!" Jake acknowledges. "Everything goes wrong on morning tour."

The aromatic smell of fresh-brewed coffee braces a mental toughness he is determined to project. Random clouds, reflecting dawn's first light on their morning edges, helps him appreciate the start of another day on Drill Platform Clybourne, one of the few active oil drill rigs still operating off the golden coast of Santa Barbara. Forty-six years drilling the modern world's oilfields have prepared Jake to handle this manmade island on stilts. Confidant, his private thoughts find comfort in the isolated lifestyle adopted years ago. His working-man's career is about over. It has been a challenge . . . and he loves it to the bone.

Drilling for oil, secreted in deep underwater formations, requires an awareness and technique similar to making love to a fine woman. Jake has no qualms viewing the oil drilling business in this manner. Those working for him know they are held accountable during this imagined act of love with the earth. The generator's hum and an occasional shudder through the lone derrick mast pointed skyward serves to indicate all is well on this phallic symbol he and his crews regard as their temporary home, temporary in the sense that oil platforms are removed from the seascape after oil and natural gas wells are depleted.

For now, life remains a constant alert where offshore rigs are concerned. Reflexes, trained for survival, send workers down toward the water in the event of fire, unless a station is assigned. Hydrogen sulfide gas—and it's up to airtight chambers and oxygen masks. Beards can't be allowed. Masks that fit tight offer better chances for survival. Tough rules . . . and inflexible.

This past week we are drilling extremely hard geologic formations with high pressure gas zones. Warning signals punctuate hectic day/night drilling activity. Platform personnel carry a mask or have it close at hand for instant use. First, there's the unmistakable odor of rotten egg. In seconds, not a trace of odor will be detected—and death follows, swift and certain.

While emergency awareness is important, it must be remembered that oil production is the primary purpose for our being here. Tight drilling schedules, with the ongoing threat of escaping gas on this well, are causing more than the normal tension. Company policies that demand week on/week off drilling with twelve hour shifts are not helping Jake maintain control. If he harbors any self doubt, he has determined, the crews will never see it.

Despite his mindset, Jake's immediate concern is captive to the luck of the draw—his least favored driller and crew are posted on the schedule board to work morning tour. Chills move through his spine when the thought occurs to him through a long workday.

Jake's concern over this particular crew is based more on instinct than fact. Charlie Adams proved himself a competent driller in California's oilfields for more than thirty years. For Jake, it's a simple reaction—when things go wrong, more often than not, it's Charlie's signature at the bottom of the report. Conversations among some drillers refer to him as "Tough Luck" Charlie, a point not lost on Jake Davis. Not admitting to being superstitious, Jake still listens to his heart: *To avoid bein' snake-bit, stand clear of the man carryin' snakes in his pocket.*

Later, with sunset painting the Pacific's horizon, Jake works to hide his anxieties while listening to the casual bantering between the changing tours. The work shift change lightens his mood as he and Charlie begin their briefing for this coming morning tour.

Jake, rarely using a man's first name on the job, distances himself slightly more in deference to Charlie's history. "Mr. Driller," Jake's unblinking eyes work to lock-in Charlie's concentration, "this well's threatening performance has kept our day tour jumping. They've been adding clay to the drilling mud all afternoon. Check it carefully, we may need to add more to shore up the walls and cool down the drill bit." After a fifteen minute summary, he orders, "Wake me up with your progress report every hour. Give me down-hole pressure and any unusual show of sour gas. Is that clear, Mr. Driller?"

Content his main point is established—that this well had better be on everyone's mind, constantly—Jake turns his attention from Charlie to stacks of reports and daily forms burying his desk. Feeling the awkward void, Charlie is left to view the back of Jake's turned head.

"Sure, Jake!" Charlie finally speaks up, irked over Jake's insulated attitude. He stares at Jake's turned head before concluding, "I'd a' done that anyhow, Jake. Hell! This well's got all of us strung out." He pauses. Sensing he can do nothing more, Charlie shrugs it off. Leaves to join his morning tour crew.

Charlie's men, noting his frustration, tease him hard about how well he has their supervisor wrapped around his little finger. Motioning them to his side for a pep talk, Charlie informs them, "Jake has a lot on his mind right now and our welfare is right there at the top. This well kept the day tour jumpin' so keep your eyes an' noses open." He is determined to face down the "tough luck" nemesis once and for all.

Jake, resuming his climb up the mound of never-ending paperwork, chuckles quietly while adding details calculated to drive shore-bound paper shufflers to distraction. Days will be spent separating these "fly specs out a' the buckwheat." Passive aggression aimed at their headquarters' detail nerds. Jake is relaxed. Even beginning to enjoy this evening's work. *Maybe "tough luck" is on a holiday.* Jake's thoughts silently allow himself the luxury of hope.

In this divining moment, Jake turns. Observes his "tool pusher" at the other end of the office, enjoying the sight of others taking the heat. "Where's our directional man?" Jake speaks up, jolting his foreman as the klaxon had earlier. "Haven't seen him all day," Jake continues. "He's s'pposed t'be reportin' regularly when we're drillin'. Is that right, Mr. Toolpusher?"

Jim, caught in the crosshairs of Jake Davis' sardonic glare, is on the spot. Not a place to be at the start of a tough Clybourne work shift. Struggling to maintain his equilibrium, Jim quickly assesses what must be done. Then quietly moves to solve the problem.

Jim Hines, in his late thirties, is a steady veteran with five years offshore drilling experience. He's aware he should have checked this before Jake called it to his attention. The only acceptable defense now is to grab a hard hat, vacate the room, and set everything straight. Anything to avoid the blistering that usually accompanies this boss' glare.

Leaving word with their dispatcher, Jim quickly moves down multiple flights of stairs to locate and deal with the directional-man problem himself. Cooling breezes, passing through the open derrick, caress his face. Nerves, rubbed raw with Jake's rough-edged treatment, relax as lights from Santa Barbara shimmer across dark, undulating water. It helps settle his mind to deal with his problem at the lowest level of the Clybourne, next to the water.

Thoughts of the woman in his life, and their two boys, asleep under those sparkling city lights, cut him some slack. The shadowed outline of the Santa Inez Mountains, made visible by myriads of blinking stars in the clear-night air, backlights a city whose beauty is rivaled by few.

Concentrate! Jim goads himself. *Where is your directional man?*

"Mac! Hey, Mac!" Mildly alarmed at not immediately sighting him in action on this lower level, Jim strains to spot Mac in dim lighting more suited to warding off passing ships than to work lights. Slurping sounds, as the sea rises through crustacean choked pilings, change to hissing sounds when sluicing back into the sea and form a foreboding answer. Straining to see, Jim studies the drill slot area being used by our rig several stories above. Mac should be here, listening to the sounds of our drilling through a stethoscope. Metal cutting sounds could indicate we are drilling through a gas production casing known to be near our bore. The resulting blast would probably mean the violent destruction of the Clybourne. *At least it would end complaints of local conservationists over our platform blighting their seascape,* Jim muses, silently.

He sights Mac, face down on the grid! "Oh my god!" Jim gasps. Sniffing the air for gas, detecting none, he moves rapidly as safety permits toward the fallen figure, pulling up short at the sound of Mac's grumbling. Fishing! The old goat is struggling to pull a ten-pound fish through a five-pound opening in the floor grid. Ludicrous!

Jim, resisting a first reaction—to boot the old man into the Pacific for such a serious mental lapse—settles for roaring laughter to calm his fury.

"Cookie's gonna skin me when he sees what I done to his fish," Mac laments, feebly holding up his stretched-out, mutilated catch. Jim wastes no time making him aware how serious this breach of the safety code is—that it will likely cost him his job.

"Cookie, my foot!" Jim continues to dress him down. "Mac, we are drilling right now. You are *supposed* to be monitoring our progress. Throw your stinking trophy to the sharks and get back on that stethoscope! You get on the phone to Jake or me every fifteen minutes. Miss one call, and I send Jake down here to deal directly with you. Face him or walk on water. The mood he's in, you know which I'd choose."

It is already settled in Jim's mind. Mac's possessions will be on the next crew boat heading ashore, his Clybourne oilfield career at an end.

***

Anger alone sustains Jim up the flights of stairs. The elevator to the drill floor, he skips. Anything to avoid facing Jake any sooner than necessary.

Sixty-year-old Jake can still knock sense into, or out of, most crewmen. A heavy-spring handgrip exerciser, crushed flat in Jake's hand, is noticed by Jim while attempting to pass, unobserved, behind the man.

"Well?" Jake asks, expecting a concise answer to all questions.

"They weren't biting!" Jim answers, hustling through the door to the drill floor, not hazarding a look in Jake's direction. You can bet the driller's first report will be in Jake's hands on time. Jim will see to that.

***

The usual trace of gas greets Jim's nose as he and the driller exchange glances, acknowledging his presence on the work floor. Things appear normal to Jim's searching eye. Drilling through tool destroying chert formations, cretaceous rock strata harder than flint, grinds our drill bits to powder these past several days. "We'll need to run a trip to replace the drill bit when you pick up your next joint," Jim yells. "How soon is that, Charlie?"

"About 0100!" Driller shouts over the rotary table's clatter. Protesting groans from the crew nearly drown out the work noise. They will labor like demons possessed, pulling heavy drill pipe out of the open hole, stack it in the derrick in ninety-foot sections, exchange the drill bit, then run it all back down hole to resume drilling. Every work crew tries to stall long enough to make the next tour do the job.

Feigning surprise at their response, Jim calls out, "Hey! Worms! That's what you get your pay for." A knowing smile is barely concealed while entering the drill shack. Jim senses five pairs of eyes penetrating his back and the obscene gesture he is certain followed their moaning. Not that long ago he would have been on their side of the gesture.

Report completed, Jim returns to the office and can't ignore Jake's quizzical expression. It forces Jim to strain the seams of his laugh control center as his boss blandly asks, "What d'ya mean, 'They ain't bitin'?'"

***

Drilling platforms were not designed with sleeping comfort in mind. Oil wells have their way to deny sleep for those having anything to do with them. Sleep is a luxury for Jake. He grabs it. Hoards it like money. Accepts being rudely woken at any hour. One pleasure remains, buoying up his spirits: the intimidating effect his voice has on drillers calling in mandatory reports.

"Yeah!" Jake shouts through the phone. "How's it look, Mr. Driller?"

The strain and discomfort in his driller's voice is almost tangible, "We're about half way out a' the hole, Jake," Charlie announces. "Barely got forty feet a' hole with the last drill bit. Jake, there is some gas pressure buildin' up below the bit right now. What d'ya think?"

No one waits long for a Jake Davis recommendation or opinion and Charlie is not kept waiting now: "Can you circulate the mud?" Jake asks.

Given an affirmative answer, Jake continues, "Add weight to the drillin' mud. Circulate the heavy stuff for forty minutes. Call me when you got it done."

While the mud man works enough weight into the drilling mud to counter rising gas pressure, Charlie and the crew rig up the kelly to pump new, heavier mud below the drill bit to stop escaping gas. His experienced crewmen know they are on the thin edge of a blowout. Good at their jobs, everything is done the way Jake knew they would. Understanding Charlie and his men need this time for proving themselves, Jake tries going back to sleep.

Rigging up the kelly goes smoothly and Charlie sends the crew on a relief break while he and the mud man finish their parts in the operation. A few hands eat lunch. Some have a smoke in the designated area.

None could have anticipated the effect these simple acts would have on their futures.

Traditionally, the least experienced hand, a "worm," is assigned to watch the controls while the driller attends to some paperwork. Barely perceptible, pipe is slowly rising out of the hole. Not certain what he is witnessing, the new man delays calling this to Charlie's attention until it nears eye level.

"Charlie, does this look right to you?" His shaky voice exposes concern. Charlie's ruddy complexion pales instantly! He recognizes the problem. This well bore is building gas pressure a lot faster than anyone anticipated. Every one of his thirty years of experience is about to be tested!

No time for consulting with Jake. It's Charlie's ass on the line. The kelly is cranked up to pump partially mixed heavy mud down the rising drill string as rapidly as the system will allow to counter escaping gas. That fails! The giant elevator hook, with the combined weight of the kelly, several tons of steel, is laid against the rising drill string in his attempt to force the pipe back down. It stops—then, agonizingly, slowly begins to push the entire mass of drill pipe, even with the added mud weight, inexorably toward the crown block at the top of the derrick mast!

Shocked at the failure of both these emergency procedures, Charlie sends the new man off the drill floor. The drill string is cut loose and the blowout protector, his last resort, is tripped. Klaxon warning signals shatter the night.

"Call Jake! Call Jim!" He yells toward the man rushing to escape.

Returning to his own problems, Charlie steels himself, trying to remain calm when it's panic clawing its way into his gut. The last anyone will recall, Charlie was at the control panel when the shades to hell violently rip open.

Jake, up in seconds, calls out orders by the book. "Everyone, get those masks on!" "Hit the alarm for back-up crew!" "Alert the fire team!"

"Where's Jim?" A first name is used without realizing he'd done it!

"Right here, Jake!" Jim reports, waiting for his next order.

"Tell dispatcher to alert all hands on the platform, Jim. Get everyone to their assigned stations and the rest to a safe area!" Jake's controlled actions calm everyone. He seems to be everywhere at once.

"Should we alert the shore?" Jim questions.

"Give us fifteen minutes to work this thing ourselves," Jake shouts, adding, "then you just handle it the way you know is right." A first time for Jake, delegating authority to make emergency decisions. Jim takes note. Respectfully vows not to let this man down.

Shrieking. Bulging. Rapidly expanding gas-filled mud powers out of the bore. It resembles a mass of bubblegum blown by a vengeful underground giant. Halfway up the derrick the mud bubble bursts, falling back, covering the work floor area with warm, wet mud. Instantaneously, huge twisting waves of flaming gas thunder through the rotary table. It blasts churning smoke and flames toward and beyond the crown block, knocking out the blinking navigational light atop the derrick and continues to boil and howl in flames above until, fuel exhausted, the drill floor plunges into smoky, eerie darkness.

Then . . . Silence! Ear drum straining silence.

Stunned, Jake and his men helplessly stand by. The blast they anticipate will be the one certain to destroy them all and whatever they hoped to be. . . . Breathless! They wait. No fire! THERE IS NO FIRE!

Death has stared them down. Backed away, without reason or excuse.

They stand as survivors. The "why" of it all—most never find an answer for this reprieve. To others, it is shrugged off. Philosophically considered "providence"!

"Jesus!" Jim forces himself to exhale. How long can a man hold his breath? It feels as though he has taken a solid kick to the chest!

"Looks like the blowout protector's doin' its job," Jake observes, after finding his voice. He orders auxiliary lights set in place while Jim takes on the duty of directing the fire crew's search for survivors or victims around a drill rig floor now wearing a blanket of scorched mud several inches thick.

With only a trace of gas being detected, everyone moves closer, assessing the damage. A headcount confirms: only the driller is missing. Last seen, he doggedly manned the control panel while a young helper left the work floor. Steam is forming. Chilled sea air, mixing with warm air off scorched and thickening drill mud, produces a smog atmosphere around the site of their missing man. Most of the work hands, joined by curious spectators, begin gathering in this general area.

Jake's body begins to shake involuntarily. He's exhausted. If all that fire hasn't done in his driller the mud or gas probably has. Remorse he senses for his attitude toward a man he spent little time to understand.

No one is allowed direct access to the real Jake Davis. They see only what he chooses to reveal. Massive deaths, witnessed during the war, should have prepared him for this. Charlie's is affecting him differently. Charlie is flesh and blood with a wife and three kids Jake will be obligated to face. How shallow now to tell them how their dad sent his crew out of harm's way. He's a hero!

Jake has much to sort out, with little time to do it. Minutes have passed. Ten, fifteen at most, since the blowout began. Confirming the exact time with Jim and others, Jake reports this incident to headquarters and requests assistance. Areas are assigned to assess damage. Groups gathering to share missed details will avoid the direct use of Charlie's name, an exercise adopted to keep a calamity impersonal. Jake knows the nature of their reactions. He understands this narrowest of escapes will remain deep inside them all for the rest of their lives.

Shouting! A fireman's voice from the work floor area freezes the men in place. Under the brake works, near the control panel site of the missing man, movement under stiffening mud is detected. Enough air trapped, enough mud cover protection from fire and gas provided to cause conditions for a verifiable miracle.

Blinded by mud, struggling to free himself, Charlie emerges. A scene all story-telling witnesses will describe as "The Mud Monster of Derrick 5-D."

"Shit!" It's Charlie's muffled voice. "Get me out a' here," he pleads.

A quick examination and wash down, and there's not a scorched hair on his body! A life spared through the miracle of a wet-mud cocoon. Jake cries out, "Ain't no butterfly ever goin' t'be prettier in my eye than Charlie is right this minute." Tears are shed on this night by some very strong men.

***

There are reports to file: hearings, inquiries, investigations by committee. God knows how many. One evident result: Jake's metamorphic change. Charlie will become Jake's life-long friend and, in a while, a business associate. The derrick—operational in something over a month. Not one person is lost or seriously injured. Humanity and Santa Barbara has avoided the sobering consequences of another blowout and oil spill.

The work crews will all recall Charlie and Jake walking together toward the aid station. Charlie, wrapped in a steaming blanket, Jake's arm around his shoulders, engaging the man in conversation: "Charlie! I'm aware I ordered you to wake me each hour. Nobody denies you did *that* tonight, but just where the hell is your report?" And the men recall Charlie's hand, barely visible under the blanket, as he responds to Jake's humor with "the finger"!

Jim Hines observed later, "This marks the first time in a ten year work relationship that Charlie has the last word in a Jake Davis conversation."

After the helicopter lifts off, transporting Charlie to the hospital, Jake stands alone near the infirmary to contemplate a rising sun breeching coastal hills and adding color to the morning's fair weather clouds. Another night has been outlasted. "Everything goes wrong on 'Morning Tour'—almost!"

***

A writer's note is appropriate regarding the Clybourne account:

The report sheet states there were no injuries in the incident. As it turned out, Charlie no longer was able to handle the strain of offshore drilling work. World Oil assigned him to their main office where he dutifully attempted to perform for nearly two months. However, years in the field had taken their toll on Charlie. He felt out of place in an office routine and was awarded a land rig assignment. This was where he discovered the enthusiasm and zeal for the oil business was gone. The Clybourne incident had taken its toll. Charlie had been "snake bit" for the last time in the oilfield.

Snake bit: Ranch and farm hands were routinely dismissed, "run off," after a snake bite. They could never again keep their minds on their jobs, it was felt. The threat of another snake bite renders them accident prone, disrupting the rest of the work crew. The oil field simply adopted and extended that same rule.

Irene Clifford

I retired two years ago and I'm having a ball just enjoying the time to do the things I always enjoyed. I love music and writing. My mother wrote a short poem on her calendar every day of her working life, so at least in volume I should be able to do something.

I've been a single mother for what seems forever and so my life choices have been dictated by the question, "Will I have benefits for my family?"

I believe I'm writing a novella, my characters have forced me into it. I've learned a lot about myself in the process, and that, of course, I need to do. When I write privately I may have to destroy it, or at least change my name to protect the innocent.

Andy

Edie was twelve. Tall, could easily have passed for sixteen. Gazing out the kitchen window as she did the dishes she felt a peace she knew wouldn't last. The grass was just starting to show a little green, a gentle breeze blew the clothes her mother already had hanging on the line. A few green buds were braving the still brisk air as spring fought for the first warm days. She thought, sadly, *if only I lived here by myself. I'd sing and fix my hair any way I wanted to and no one would ever come in the house unless I invited them.*

"Hurry up with those dishes. By the time you finish them it'll be lunch," called her mother, Clare, from the living room. She knew how Edie loved to daydream. She had a private world. None of them could intrude.

Edie was the oldest of four. That was a lot of hungry people come dinnertime.

"Ah, Baby, you heard your mother tell ya, hurry up with those dishes, and how about some coffee for your old man?" said Ray as he pressed her into the sink causing her to get her little tummy wet.

"Stop it Daddy. I'm hurrying. Don't push on me."

"Leave that girl alone," snapped Clare as she hurried into the kitchen. "What's wrong with you? She's just a kid."

"Ah, I'm only playing with her," answered Ray as he patted Clare's bottom and poured himself a cup of coffee.

Edie could feel her heart pounding. She hurried through the dishes and left the kitchen without even glancing at her father.

"You spoil Edie, make her think she's somethin' special. What she is is a stuck-up little brat. Well, she'll get her comeuppance one of these days. She'll never get a husband if she don't learn that a man is the boss. A little caterin' would be a good thing for her to learn."

Edie knew everything her father would be saying as if she had the door open. Everything but the truth. Sunday after Sunday they sat like pious little puritans in that Methodist Church her mother thought of as her second home. She bet that when Ray was down on his knees confessing his sins to our almighty father he never mentioned how he touched her breast every time he passed her in their narrow hall. Or, the day he'd left the bathroom door open, called her and then let her see his "thing." She had been disgusted and run away. Then life in the house only got worse. He'd press his heavy body against her whenever there was an opportunity. She stuck to her mom's side like a Siamese twin. Ray kept giving her that funny look of his. The first night he came into her room he'd started by saying they should get to be friends. He didn't mean to upset her all the time. He'd stroked her body, her hair, told her how beautiful she was. Edie had actually liked it a little. She felt ashamed. Then he had put his "thing" in her. It hurt. She cried. He said he felt she liked it. Good. He'd be back again. "Don't even think about telling your mom. If you do, forget about ever getting yourself a boyfriend."

Edie managed to stay away from Ray much more than he thought she'd be able too. She devised reasons to stay with a girlfriend for a night, or sleep with one of the younger children who suddenly seemed to have nightmares. Edie felt that her mom knew how Ray tormented her, but she was afraid of him. They all were.

School was the only place she found release. Although almost painfully shy, Edie enjoyed the safety of numbers. Here, at least, her father could not torment her with his incessant pawing and constant teasing. And then to have one of the most sought after boys in the senior class pay attention to her, school was not only her refuge but her heaven. *From hell to heaven,* she sometimes thought and wished her father dead.

That first date—how clearly she remembered every detail. Alex breathless from chasing her down after class and asking in that nice way he had, *would you like to go to a show with me sometime. Sure thing,* Edie had answered in the calmest voice she could muster. *Would I like it, geese, do birds fly?* Of course that wasn't included in her answer.

She dressed so carefully for that first date. Pretty feminine dress, the type a man would like. Edie knew she had a good body, she had heard her father tell her mother that she'd come to no good. "That girl's built like a brick shit house." Didn't sound to great to her, but she got the idea. Edie felt she'd only get the one chance to favorably impress Alex and she figured she'd just tease him enough so he'd ask her out again and again. She really liked him and it didn't hurt that he was smart, would probably always have a good job, plus, his family had money. The only way to get out of the little town she was anchored to would be to marry out of it. Everything went well on their first date. They kissed, she rubbed her breasts against his arm. Once she even managed to hug him from behind. He'd been so excited but had managed to be a gentleman all the same. Next date was scheduled for the next day, Saturday. They'd gone for something to eat and some more necking. Edie was deliriously happy. She found herself in love and truly enjoyed the sensation. When they kissed, she was flooded with heat, but she never gave in to the desires of her body. As she told Alex, only her husband would be the man to "go all the way" with her.

Quickly the summer passed and through tears and promises of love forever, Alex left for college. And they were true to each other, he because he was much too shy and faithful to do anything different and Edie because her whole dream was to be Alex's wife. She dreamt of the day he would call and ask her to be his for the rest of their lives. Finally it happened.

Royal L. Craig

I started writing poetry in first grade at school. I was promptly accused of plagiarism. I went underground with my writing for years.

I have been writing in poetry, essays, short stories, non-fiction, and a number of failed attempts at novels. My writing is eclectic, covering a wide range of subjects. I refuse to be tied down to what is referred to as commercial writing. I write where the spirit takes me, and to hell with the consequences. The writing opportunity provided by the workshop has been a godsend for me, as it also stresses points generally not covered by conventional teachings.

My awards and publications are not great in number: The Oregon State Poetry Association, The US Post Office Healthy Aging Award, California State Poetry Society, Lynx, Epic Publishing Co., Tebot Bach.

Often, it is with one's grandparents that one finds the comfort that parents sometimes neglect in their pursuit of making a home. Here, the poet as a child loses his close friend who understands everything.

Fishing

That morning you died, Grandfather,
I thought the world had lost its pivot.
Emptiness swept in like a silent wind
With your strangely pale form on the bed,
And the window curtains drawn.
Dispossessed of meaning,
I ran from the weeping house
Down to the river,
To sit on the old willow tree
Sloping over the deep pool
Where you had taught me to fish
On my fifth birthday.
I glanced over
To the far gravel bank
Where you loved to cast your line
Knee deep to your waders,
And there you were!
Your line stretched out
Over the running water,
Your rod bent to the splash of a trout.
Working it to your side,
You released it back to freedom
From your barbless hook.
You looked over at me and winked
Like you always did,

Then you began to fade
As you whipped the line
Out over the flowing stream.
Somehow I knew
You had cast the line for me
And caught me, and let me go
With a wink—painlessly
Back into the world again.

Interstices

I

Brinnell carefully lifted the flap of the one-man tent he had camouflaged with tree branches and peered out apprehensively. There was mist on the slopes of the foothills, and the air had a cold edge. He searched for any sign of activity down the trail. There was no movement, no sound of voices. Staggering to his feet, he popped his head out of the tent opening. He slipped into blue jeans and denim jacket, and stepped outside to relieve a sudden need. The cold wet grass on his bare feet drove the sleep from his head. The chilly morning stillness was intensified by the soft chirping of buntings in a nearby thicket. A bushy tailed squirrel, perched on a pine branch, was twitching and turning, alarmed at his intrusion. He scanned the valley for any sign of human life, but again, nothing. It was heavily forested, and he found it difficult to see beyond the canopy. Overhead he spied an eagle, riding the updraft from the early morning sun. There was something exhilarating in its effortless flight, its occasional stroke of wings. Brinnell watched the raptor, and his caution gave way to a sudden flush of joy, that he was back once more in mountain terrain.

Stretched out before him down the slope were aspen and willow trees tipped with the light virgin green of early spring, the line of misty hills, the river tumbling down the rocky valley below and the snow tipped mountain high above. 'Here, I could die content.' The thought came spontaneously to his mind, and he chuckled, murmuring, "Well, live, anyway."

At the far end of the valley, he noticed a wispy curl of smoke rising in the still air—the start of a forest fire, or a campfire, some twenty miles away. In either case he had to get going. He finished dressing. Packing his worn duffle and back-pack, Brinnell broke out a bar of nuts and seeds and began chewing the stubborn thing, all the while contemplating his situation. He was thankful that he was tall, thin, and muscular, and an experienced mountain climber. He was, however, disturbed by that smoke in the valley. Was he being shadowed? They seemed to be persistently on his trail. Who were they, and what did they want? Thinking back to the triumphs and the tragedy at Mt. Cho Oyo in Tibet, he recalled how some had conquered, a few had failed, one fatally. Was it the brother of the one who had fallen tragically, the brother who had blamed him when the piton gave way? The price of conquest was, on occasion, very high, but the rewards made one feel vibrantly alive and worth the risk. Perhaps he should wait and confront them. He finally decided—let them stew; he wasn't responsible for the death, no matter what they thought. He was secure in his skills, and felt that he could lose them easily when the going got tough. Here he was, back in sierra country, away from noise, people, automobiles, and ceaseless activity, and certain other things. There were things he didn't like to think about, things he couldn't forget.

Images—like the day he thought he spotted his beautiful Natasha on Roosevelt Ave. by the university. She was just jaunting along, her usual carefree self, in a gray tweed mountain climbing outfit with an alpine hat set at a jaunty angle. He called to her, but she disappeared in the crowd. Not sure of what he had seen, Brinnell was surprised when she appeared again later. She was suddenly there, in the crowded elevator at the Space Needle, in a tied-at-the waist open blue shirt. He tried to reach her as the doors opened, but she turned a corner and disappeared. He searched the rotating restaurant on top, but never found her. It had to have been an illusion. He realized he still missed her. A lot! They were good together. It had been a few years since they were together, but the animal attraction and deep affection remained. He wondered if she had ever gotten married, then caught himself, putting regrets and longings out of his mind.

With renewed vigor, he headed into the last of the foothills, fighting his way through bracken and thick undergrowth. Later, he came upon a forest clearing with a huge, gray granite rock. It provided a vantage point to view the trail back, and he clambered up. He scanned the misty, tree-covered flank of the foothill he had traveled through yesterday. There was no movement. He listened intently, cocking his calloused hands behind deeply tanned ears. Was that the faint sound of voices in the distance? He couldn't be certain, but instinct told him to keep moving. He turned to consider a narrow animal path leading higher up the hill. Or become clever. He decided to try clever. On the far side of his rock, he had noticed a stream burbling down the hill. He slid carefully down the slope of the rock into the small stream. Trying not to disturb any stone that would betray his passing, he plodded upstream through thick brush that eventually gave way to spruce and pine. His hiking boots were slipping and sliding on wet round stones in spite of his care. Brinnell's tension gradually began to relax. It was doubtful anyone could follow his trail now.

He came to the edge of a sloping meadow covered in daisies and bluebells in among grasses and low shrubs. He rested and took a swig of cool water from the canteen. The sky was a deeper blue than he remembered. He watched a tuft of cloud tearing itself from the leeside of the mountain top up ahead. He would not be found easily up there. He rose and approached a swale with tall reedy grasses and bulrushes by a large pond fed by his stream. He disturbed a blue heron, which flew up, making a long sweep to a spot further down the stream. He went round the pond and up a little further to the stream's source—a clear spring in a rocky depression. He refilled his canteen, and then sank down on the grass, resting his head on his pack, and pulling his camouflaged peaked hat over his eyes.

Later he heard a sound and caught a movement out of one eye. He sat up, startled! It was Natasha, young, beautiful, blond, washing her body at the edge of the pond he had passed. Not Natasha again! Brinnell was stricken again with her beauty. He watched her, enraptured at the scene. He started to approach, but thought he might frighten her; she may not be Natasha. He reclined again, and nonchalantly called out to her, "Hello." She looked up and smiled, and went on washing her legs. Emboldened, Brinnell rose and moved towards her.

Was it her? Stepping out of the water, she moved out beyond the tall grass, with towels in one hand. Her body was beautifully molded, her flowing blond hair all down on one side, playing peek-a-boo with one breast. She smiled and said, "Hello, Brunie. Isn't this a beautiful day?" Only Natasha had ever called him that, but it couldn't be. How could she be up here all alone?

Nonplussed, he said, "How do you know that name? Aren't you chilly in this air?"

"It's not chilly. Do you think I could forget your name? Come on! Don't tell me you don't remember me. We were lovers. Remember? That afternoon at the Pike, that night on the beach, just you and I, our many nights together."

Brinnell blurted out, "But that was some time ago. Are you really Natasha, you can't be. She's probably married by now and living down in California. But if you are not my Natasha, you look exactly like her."

Was this the woman from whom he had fled that sorrowful time a few years ago? Natasha, stunningly beautiful, very feminine, had been his trophy to wear on his arm, the envy of his friends.

She pouted and said, "I am the one you loved and left, with nowhere to turn."

Brinnell's mind flew back to that time with Natasha. He was younger then, thin and brash and self-important. He remembered how desirable she had looked that languorous evening on the beach, on Monterey Bay, under the palm trees. Together they had watched the sun's decline, firing the sky with a throbbing red. They had been lying side by side for a long while, but eventually Nature had her way with them; and in ecstatic, passionate embrace, they had stormed the gates of heaven. It is often said that the flame that brightly burns, quickly dies, and their nights of passion never reached the heights of that first embrace. But she was his emblem, ever at his side, ever affirming his macho image.

He recalled her disclosure later that she was with child. His only question, "And . . . am I the father?" It was some time before she answered, "Of course." The last thing Brinnell wanted in his roaming life was the responsibility of a child, or horrors, a wife. Her hesitancy and controlled response had been a shock; it was possibly not even his child. He had brought her an Irish setter puppy as a present for the baby. The thought of this entanglement in his bachelor life style had filled him with dread. He had left and joined a climbing group for Tibet and Mt. Cho Oyo.

"And the baby, what happened to the baby?"

She eyed him sadly, and then said, "The baby? Abortion! Poor Brunie, you disappeared before I could assure you it was yours."

"But I asked, you didn't answer."

"I had to think how it would affect you, affect us being together. I suspected a bad reaction. I knew you liked your independent life style. You behaved badly. I couldn't care for it alone, I was broke."

Natasha bent over one leg, drying her body. She rose slowly and toweled her upper body, massaging her glistening breasts provocatively, slowly drying one, then the other. Brinnell's tanned face flushed red with his confusion, resurgent memory, and erotic impulse. He finally found his voice, "But that was over six years ago."

She pouted, teasingly, "That was only yesterday. You have such a bad memory."

"What are you doing here? Are you alone up here in this mountain?"

"I am with you. Aren't you happy to see me? Come here, sit with me."

Natasha spread a beach towel on the grass, and reclined, stretching out, smiling sweetly. In his consternation, Brinnell tried to gather his thoughts, his face a furrowed study. Who was this woman? Strange as hell, his Natasha had come back to him. He muttered to himself, "Just enjoy."

Slowly he turned his gaze to her, to where she was lying. She was not there! He looked around; she was slowly walking up a narrow trail, a towel over her shoulder, and another around her waist. She turned and smiled, and was gone! The area was empty except for a minnow rising to a mosquito on the surface of the pond. There were just tall grasses and bulrushes nodding in the slight breeze, no Natasha, no towels. Only the grass flattened where she had been lying. He sagged down, bewildered. Was that a dream? Had he been hallucinating? No! It happened! Look! The grass is flattened where she was. Proof! That's proof! Proof of what? He started to go after her, but realized she had to be an illusion. More confused than ever, Brinnell went back to his pack and shouldered it. He half muttered to himself, "She lied, there was no baby." He desperately wanted to believe his thoughts, not her words. Troubled with lingering regret, he turned onto the same uphill trail she had taken and began the ascent. He thought he saw movement on the back trail, and in the distance, the very faint sound of voices—he just knew this was going to be a long day.

2

The path was becoming arduous, and Brinnell spied a stalwart ash sapling in among a stand of deciduous trees. Slipping his camp axe from its holster, he cut the sapling to about a six-foot length, and trimmed it of its branches. He hefted his new stave, and satisfied, returned to climbing up wet loose shale with its slippery patches of moss. By late afternoon the path leveled off. He approached the edge of a shear cliff, one face of a steep gorge. There seemed to be no way to get across. Higher up, it looked as if the gorge might narrow, so he turned and renewed the climb. Brinnell was beginning to tire. He had no schedule to keep, and it was getting late enough to consider making camp for the night. He came to a clean rocky ledge overlooking the gorge which also gave him a clear view of the trail back and broke out his tent. He wanted no surprises, just a night of rest and forgetfulness. There would be no campfire this night to give away his position. The sun was getting lower, and the chilling breeze across the ledge refreshed him, but it was going to be a cold night. Unwrapping a ration of dried fruit and hard biscuits, he snacked desultorily, drinking from his canteen, reviewing, and trying to make sense of the day's happenings—the sudden appearance and disappearance of Natasha. It had to be a madcap delusion; his Natasha had long gone out of his life, or so he thought.

"Are you lost?"

Startled, Brinnell looked up. Lost in thought, he hadn't noticed a child standing a few feet in front him. "No. Who are you?"

"I am your little girl, Tanya."

"But I never had a little girl." He figured her to be five or six years of age. She was beautiful, with shoulder length blond curls and sparkling sky-blue eyes. She wore a rose-flowered white dress with a stained yellow pinafore, white anklets, and black strapped sandals.

"Yes you did! Then you ran away! Don't you remember?"

Bewildered, Brinnell didn't respond. "Was your mommy's name, Natasha?"

"Not was, silly! Is! My mom is Natasha. She's alive, you know."

"Where do you live? Where is your mommy now?"

"She's home."

"Where's home? How did you get your dress dirty?"

"It's a pinafore. I've been playing with Polcan."

"What's Polcan?"

"My dog. You should know; you got him for my birthday."

Brinnell's mind began to spin. My Natasha didn't have the abortion after all. And this is the child she had—my child. But how can that be, this child—alone in these foothills. Dammit! This must be some kind of curse because I abandoned Natasha. This whole thing is an illusion! This Tanya doesn't really exist.

He turned to the girl, and asked suspiciously, "Aren't you cold? You don't seem too well-dressed for the mountains."

"I'm O.K., I'm not cold."

"Are you real? Come here and let me touch you. I don't think you're real."

Tanya advanced obediently and held out her hand to him. He took the hand, it was warm and soft and delicate. He felt a sudden rush of emotion. A child of his he had never known was really here, standing right in front of him! He remained vigilant.

"How did you find me? Where did you come from?"

"Mommy told me where you were. I came from home." Impatiently, she added, "I told you that already."

Tanya turned and said, "I have to go now. Mommy's calling me." With that she turned and ran up the path. She looked back at Brinnell and with a little wave, said, "Goodbye," then she added, "Daddy." She was gone. Brinnell was alone. Again! He had half a mind to follow her, but still suspected she was just more of the illusion, disappearing so quickly.

He sat hunched up in his sleeping bag at the tent opening, staring into the night. What was the trick that was being played on him? It had to be some sort of hypnosis. No, that wasn't it. What was it? He remembered the soft warm touch of the child's hand and held back the impulse of an involuntary tear. He was surprised at his reaction. Was this the same man that had run away from responsibility? Could she truly be his daughter? No, not possible; this was all some kind of trick. "Big tough guy," he thought, "can't handle a stupid game being played on me." Disgusted with his weakness, he fell back and was soon sound asleep.

The raucous cawing of crows shot him awake at false dawn. Noisy and boisterous, they had congregated high in a pine tree near his tent. Looking up, he couldn't see a single one of the black noisemakers, yet there must have been over a hundred, all in loud heated argument. Then the crows suddenly fell silent. In the distance, Brinnell could hear what sounded like lapping water, or the faint sound of voices. Hurriedly he broke camp and headed up the trail, munching on a bar, half-expecting to see little Tanya running up ahead.

3

Sheriff Jimmy Kaprinski of San Jose County chewed on his stick of licorice root in lieu of a cigarette, looked at the form on the bathroom floor and said to Pat, his deputy, "It's a damn shame, that's what it is, a damn shame."

Pat was bent over the bloodstained body and the dead baby, studying the scene. She looked up at him, "Do you know her?'

"Yes, I've seen her around town on one or two occasions. I think she worked at the downtown library. It looks like an attempted abortion, but we'll see. It may have just happened by itself. Or she may have had help. Someone else may have done this to her. If so, somebody's made a dumb mistake. We'll let the coroner fill us in on the details." Jimmy turned the latch on the front door, "Call the coroner when you're finished."

The sheriff shifted his heavy frame into his car, his hands trembling, and tried to think it through. The last time he had seen Peggy, they had watched the stars coming into brightness over the harbor as the evening waned. He had suggested an abortion. "Just get it done properly at a clinic."

"Clinic! Clinic! Who needs a clinic? I am from the old country, we know things. I can take care of myself."

"Don't take any foolish chances. It's your life you're fooling with. And another thing, why won't you tell me what your real name is, anyway? God knows, I've asked you often enough. I could find out, you know."

"Don't be such a bore. You couldn't pronounce it, Peggy's a good name, don't you think?" She had patted her swollen belly, smiled at Jimmy, and said, "I have a little Jimmy in here."

"Don't talk like that! You can't be sure it's mine. You know I'd have trouble keeping it quiet in town. You've been seeing someone else, haven't you? What's his name?"

"What a guy! Always after names!"

Jimmy turned to her and said very slowly, "You know, you can't lay this on me. It's my job and my marriage on the line."

"What marriage? To Sylvia? That's no marriage. Trouble all the time. When's the last time she made love to you?" Jimmy said nothing.

She turned away, "I won't tell you who he is."

"I'll find out sooner or later, and then he and I will have a little talk."

"You are so possessive. Why are you so jealous? You want two wives? Leave things alone. Don't interfere. And take me home."

They drove back in silence. He dropped her at the parking lot at Ralph's Market. Peggy got out of the car angrily and slammed the door without a word. She buzzed her lock, got into her car, and sped out and down the street. Jimmy drove home, irritated and confused.

As the tragedy of her death repeated itself in his mind, yet a third time, Sheriff Jimmy left the house of death and drove back to the Sheriff's station, thinking, "This whole thing has to do with that guy she's been seeing. He's sure to have had a hand in this; he talked her into it. He didn't want a child either. How far did he go to make sure? If there was any foul play, he's involved. I gotta have a talk with him. This thing could get out of hand. We may be talking murder! It better not be murder. If it is, and it's her boyfriend, he's a dead man." He made his way back to the office.

Pat informed him the following week, "The coroner said it was death due to a sanguinary condition following an abortion. She must have lain there for hours before she died. The evidence did not rule out foul play." The case dribbled on, leads dried up. It became a lukewarm case until the name Stephen Brinnell came up a few years later. He had had a book overdue, and the librarian had spoken to the sheriff.

His rejoinder, "You want me to go catch someone who has a book overdue?"

Thin-lipped, she said tersely, "He was very friendly with that Peggy girl that died."

The sheriff's ears perked up at this.

"Why didn't you tell me? He demanded. Stiffly, she responded, "You never asked."

"Have you seen him lately?"

"No, otherwise I would have confronted him about the overdue."

He looked at the last date on the library record, May 5, corresponding roughly near the date of Peggy's

death. Sheriff Jimmy found this coincidence too good
to pass up.

He spoke to the deputy, "No loose ends. I want to
know if Brinnell had anything to do with that girl's
death. I want this case put to bed." A closed case meant
no questions arising about infidelity. Jimmy wanted a
closed case.

"Find out what you can about Stephen Brinnell.
Find out where he works. Find him and bring him
in."

A few days later the deputy reported, "Well, we
found him. That is, we found out who he is. He's a
wanderer, been all over the world climbing mountains.
That's where he is now, up in Washington."

Sheriff Jimmy's eyes grew beady. He said, "Find out
which mountain in Washington. Then we'll go get
him."

Pat objected, "That's out of our jurisdiction."

"You are right. I know sheriff Banes up there. We've
been on fishing trips together. I'll give him a call and
he'll make arrangements. We'll go call on this Brinnell
together."

He turned to her, "You can come along if you
like."

Pat smiled, and said, "Count me in."

4

Brinnell finally reached the apex where the gorge walls
conjoined and became solid ground. The conifers were
becoming sparse. He found it easy to cross and began

to travel laterally, partly to travel more easily, and partly to confuse anyone following his trail and guessing his intentions. Coming to a sheer granite bluff towering some two hundred feet above him, his trained eyes scanned it for a possible climb. He stopped to check his climbing gear: rope, snap rings, and pitons. He began the climb. The ascent was not easy due to water percolating down through a loose stratum of slate angling across the bluff face, but picking his way carefully, he eventually reached the top, a little tired, but content. This bluff marked the end of the foothills and the beginning of the mountain range proper. Looking back, he could see the hills rolling in deepening misty layers down to the flatlands. There was no sign of anyone following. Completely alone, Brinnell felt he was free of troubles with the past at last. The snow patched bluff was uneven on top and extended some hundreds of yards back. Regaining his strength, he resumed his trek, past small patches of ice and sparse grass, and around slippery mossy rocks. The trees were thinly scattered and were stunted in growth. He decided to make camp. Waiting for tea water to begin boiling in a tin cup on his Sterno can stove gave him time to reflect. Although it was a long time back, he now wished he had put things right with Natasha. And the daughter, his daughter! But he couldn't figure out where reality lay. She said she had had an abortion, but here she was (where, he wasn't certain) with her Tanya very much alive, or so it seemed. As he finished a light meal, sleep overcame him without a visitation or other strange event. The next morning found him eager to climb. His approach to the summit of the higher peak was along a snow-laden saddle some eight hundred feet up that swept between the peak that was his goal and a lower one. It was slow going, and late afternoon found him ready for a break. He was chewing on some hard biscuit when he spied a cabin perched on a cliff edge lower down. He felt that this saddle was subject to an avalanche, and the cabin looked precariously vulnerable to the snow field high above it. He saw a thin stream of smoke curling from its chimney. It needed closer inspection; there was someone inside. He was certain it was not those who had been dogging his trail; he had covered too much difficult terrain for them to be this close.

As he drew closer to the cabin, nevertheless, he moved quietly. He watched for a while, but there was no movement, no sound. Quietly he climbed onto the porch and listened for any sign of life inside. The sudden barking of a dog startled him. He was surprised when the storm door suddenly slammed open. Standing there was Natasha, clad in blue and white ski togs, smiling, and looking more beautiful than he remembered. She was holding the dog; it was straining at the collar.

She spoke to the dog, "Polcan, sidet, tino, svoj." She looked up at Brinnell, "It's O.K. We were beginning to wonder if you were going to make it in time."

Natasha gave him a broad smile, and added, "I'm glad you're here. Come on in. The dog won't bother you. After all, you're the one who brought him as a playmate for Tanya."

Brinnell was incredulous. "What are you doing here? How did you get here? Don't you know this is avalanche season?"

Natasha smiled coyly and said, "Yes, I know."

Polcan finally wagged its tail in greeting to Brinnell. Natasha gave her Brunie a big hug, and asked, "Won't you come in? I'll make you a nice hot toddy."

Tanya, in yellow pajamas with little pink puppy prints, peaked from behind her mother, and said, "Hi, Daddy!"

Natasha made room for him to enter and he shouldered his way past them into the rough pine structure. He looked around. The cabin consisted of one large room with two rough bunks against a wall and a rude wood table at one side, complete with four chairs made from small peeled logs and branches. There was a soft glow from the oilcan stove set in the middle of the room which was permeated with the persistent odor of smoke mixed with the scent of pine. Firewood was stacked in a corner.

He turned savagely on Natasha, "You told me you had an abortion, and here's your daughter. How did you disappear by the pond that day? You were there, and then you were gone."

Natasha didn't answer at first; she poured hot water into two cups, added sugar-coated spice sticks, shots of brandy, stirred them, and handed one to Brinnell. "I wanted Tanya to see you first, and measure your reaction."

"How could you do that? You weren't there."

"Think about it, runaway daddy, will I send my little daughter miles away from this cabin by herself?"

"You spied on us!"

Tanya began to tear up at his harsh tone.

Natasha cast her eyes in the direction of the child and said quietly to Brinnell, "Speak softly."

Ignoring her comment, Brinnell went on, "What are you, some Eskimo type? That day by the pond, it was in the 30s or low 40s, and you were washing yourself with ice water."

"Sorry, I didn't notice the temperature. Did you ever regret you left me that day?"

"And when I saw Tanya, she wasn't dressed for the mountains." He paced around the room, "What's going on?"

"Nothing is going on. I tried to meet you back in the city, but it was so crowded, you disappeared. We just want to be a family. Why don't you come live with us? I have a nice home up here in the mountains. You'll love it, it's warm and cozy, and the springtime is wonderful. All sorts of wild flowers and birds, and even bears. You'll see a lot of them when the blueberries come into season."

Brinnell felt exasperated, "Don't you know that you could be the victims of an avalanche at any moment."

Natasha said softly, "I know."

Brinnell continued, "The weather is warming and there's a snow load directly up the hill above us that could smash this cabin into kindling and knock it off this cliff. What made you want to come up here, anyway?"

"We just want to be with you. I knew you would come here, so I waited."

"How could you know? I didn't know myself until a little while ago."

"Oh Brunie, you're always so full of questions. Tell me you're glad to see me."

"Of course I am. Let's get some sleep, and we'll pack up and leave this place first thing in the morning."

Tanya had curled up in a homespun quilt with Polcan across her bed and was already asleep.

Natasha offered Brinnell the bottom bunk. "If it gets cold in the night, throw a log or two in the fire." With that, she climbed into the top bunk and threw Brinnell a kiss, "Good night, runaway lover," and closed her eyes.

Brinnell rested on the smelly quilt that passed for a mattress and was thankful that she had made no romantic offer; he was too confused by events as it was. It was very late in the night when Brinnell heard a rumble like a distant train that grew to a roar, and then suddenly all was silent. It was promptly forgotten. Brinnell was surprised by a sudden headache that as quickly disappeared. Exhausted, he fell sound asleep and didn't awaken until dawn.

Voices in the distance awakened him, and Brinnell roused the others. "Time to go!" There was snow everywhere in the cabin. Avalanche? Was that what he had heard in the night? Natasha looked more vibrant than ever. Somehow they found their way up and out. He could see four or five figures far down the hill, and

knew they would find the going tough in fresh snow.
He thought he recognized one of the group.

"That looks a little bit like Sheriff Jimmy from San
Jose, where we used to live. What could he be doing up
in these parts? What would he want with me? Or is he
looking for you?"

Natasha said, irritably, "Never mind, that's another
world. He belongs to the past, the long dead past. Let's
just get going."

Sheriff Jimmy reached the area below where the
cabin should be, and asked Joe, his tracker, "Are you
sure this is the spot?"

Joe wiped his forehead, and answered, "This is the
cabin. You are standing on top of it. That thunder we
heard last night was the avalanche sweeping down from
the saddle. It has pushed the cabin off the cliff and covered it at least twenty feet deep. There is nothing left."

Jimmy said sadly. "There was smoke coming from
the smoke stack. That meant there was somebody inside. We've got to try and see if anyone survived. I tell
you what: go down to that stand of aspen we passed
coming up here. Cut some of the longer saplings and
we'll probe the area, just in case."

The poles struck boards and shingles, but nothing softer. The search took hours, but no bodies, were
found, alive or dead.

Joe looked at Jimmy and said, "We'll have to leave
it. We're not equipped to do more. Whoever was in
that cabin is dead. You can call for help. If they want
to come up, we'll wait for them, but we won't find any-

thing here till spring." Jimmy returned the look glumly,

Sheriff Banes said, "God knows what we'll find then. But we must do what we can." He got on his radio and made the call.

Brinnell found going uphill surprisingly easy. He knew it was cold, but for some reason, he didn't feel the chill. There seemed to be a certain transparency to the terrain that he couldn't quite grasp. He felt extremely light and was surprised that he wasn't sinking into soft snow. He saw his footprints were barely visible. He felt indefatigable, and they soon arrived at the top of the saddle. He said to Natasha, "There has been an avalanche overnight. It was a good thing that it missed the cabin."

Natasha said, "You know, Brunie, you are so cute. It took a lot of persuading to get you here. This is your destiny—to be with us. I know it, and Tanya knows it a little. Polcan is just happy to be with us." She pointed to the north, "See that mountain peak? Our home is on that mountain. Let's keep going."

Brinnell stopped and stared at her, "You told me that it was here on the far side of the saddle." He pointed down into the far valley. Do you really know where we are going? Tanya will be getting tired. I am sure she will be getting hungry."

Tanya spoke up, stroking the dog, "Oh, Daddy, it's all right, I'm O.K. Mommy didn't want to tell you, but she doesn't know where our home is, not exactly." She smiled, "But anyway, we are all together."

Natasha scowled, "Enough talking. Let's just keep going. I know we'll get there soon."

Brinnell said conspiratorially to Tanya, "I think your mother is not telling us something we should know. We could wander up here forever."

Natasha smiled and said nothing.

Gerry Gooding

I grew up in rural Illinois, joined the Air Force right out of high school, and was trained as an electronics technician. My first assignment after technical school was in Okinawa, where I fell in love with the Japanese language and culture. It was a love affair that would become a lifelong passion. After 26 years in the Air Force and 10 more with an aerospace firm, I decided to try my hand at the translator trade. At the time these selections were written I had been translating technical Japanese for 15 years. Converting the thoughts of Japanese writers into English was interesting and rewarding, but I also had some important things of my own to say.

As a new participant in the senior citizen writer's workshop, I was pleased to learn that our writing need not be confined to any particular genre. I wrote a series of mildly liberal opinion articles including "The USA Patriot Act: Why all the Fuss?," "Our Cuban Prison," and "Governing by Direct Democracy." But I was not prepared for the reaction. When the group reviewed the first article (which does not appear here), I was shocked by the level of acrimony it had inspired. A week or two later, I saw one of the workshop participants in the hallway. As I approached, she averted her eyes to avoid greeting me! The ill will was even worse than I had imagined.

A member of the group took me aside to give me some friendly advice. He urged me to write fiction or memoirs, as all of the other participants were doing. I knew he was trying to preserve the congenial atmosphere of the group.

I had never seriously considered writing fiction, but decided to give it a try. I wrote "The Shady Spot" based on something that happened to me as a child. It was an important part of growing up.

Governing by Direct Democracy

Simply stated, in representative democracy, the people elect representatives to enact legislation; and in direct democracy, the people vote directly on specific issues. In California, we are depending more and more on the ballot initiative to enact our laws. This trend toward direct democracy is *not* a good thing.

We expect our lawmakers to study pending legislation, debate it, deliberate, and to make decisions only after they have done this. We the people, however, have neither the time nor the will to study the propositions we will face in the voting booth. We base our votes primarily on what we learn from television ads, mailings, and door-to-door campaigns paid for by opponents and supporters of the propositions. The side with the most money to spend wins.

Moreover, we are held accountable for our votes only to the extent that we are directly affected by resulting laws. And even when we are called to account for our actions in this manner, we seldom make the connection between the pain we are suffering and our vote that caused it. We would happily vote for one proposition to cut taxes, another to require a balanced budget, and a third to provide additional services, all on the same ballot, with nary a thought as to how this remarkable feat is to be accomplished. (Shucks, we can't do everything. What do you think those damn representatives are for?)

We enacted a "three strikes" law, thinking it would serve as a deterrent, possibly helping to alleviate the problem of overcrowded prisons. Now there is little evidence to suggest that the law acts as a deterrent; and we are now putting some petty criminals in prison for life on one hand, as we release others early to ease overcrowding on the other. We passed proposition 13 to rescue little old ladies from being forced out of their homes by rising property taxes, and we now tax Warren Buffet's beachfront property at a fraction of what his neighbors pay. On a much lower scale, a young couple moving in next door to me would pay four times the property tax I pay. Is this fair? It would not seem to be, but is it popular? The rapid response by our governor to terminate Warren's suggestion to repeal Proposition 13 suggests that it is.

Representative democracy is capable of fairness. Statesmen can, and often do, vote against the interests of the majority to protect the rights of the minority. Direct democracy, however, cannot be counted on for fairness. I feel strongly about this. I automatically vote NO on all propositions except those benefiting schools, for which I automatically vote YES. In following this policy, I probably vote for some bad propositions, and against some good ones, but over the long haul I think the policy usually ends up putting me on the right side of the issues. If we all did this, we might even return to a more representative democracy.

Our Cuban Prison

During the war in Afghanistan, the US military captured a large number of prisoners. A couple of years ago, hundreds of these prisoners were identified as "the worst of the worst." They were bound hand and foot, blindfolded, loaded onto cargo planes and transported to a prison camp at the US military base at Guantanamo Bay, Cuba, where all but a small fraction of them still remain. It is unclear how these particular prisoners were selected, but intelligence officers who were involved in their interrogation said that many had been judged to have no value as sources of intelligence, and had been recommended for release, but were taken anyway.

After several months in captivity, some forty of the prisoners were released without explanation. One of those released was an old shepherd who claimed to be 105 years old. Reporters noted that he seemed confused, and had difficulty answering simple questions. The Bush Administration also has difficulty answering simple questions such as who the prisoners are, why they are being held, and what is in store for them.

Under the Geneva Conventions, such basic information about prisoners of war must be released. But Secretary of Defense Donald Rumsfeld has said that these men are not prisoners of war; they are enemy combatants. The Conventions, however, require that all prisoners captured in wartime be treated as prisoners of war until their status can be ascertained by a military tribunal. In Guantanamo, the status of the prisoners appears to have been determined by general decree.

We do know that the prisoners are nationals of over forty countries, including the U.K., Australia, and Belgium. This collection of the "worst of the worst" also includes boys between the ages of 13 and 16. Prison officials report that the boys have been separated from the adult prisoners. Unlike the adult prisoners, who are kept in individual 6- by 8-foot chain link cages, the teenagers have spacious quarters with recreational facilities. They are well-fed, and are being taught to read and write their native language. Prison officials say the boys are far better off now than they were before they were captured. Amnesty International, however, insists that the US is violating the UN Convention on the Rights of the Child, which states that "every child deprived of his or her liberty shall have the right to prompt access to legal and other appropriate assistance."

The parents of twelve Kuwaiti prisoners have pooled their resources and hired attorneys to attempt to get a hearing for their sons. They spent about two million dollars in an unsuccessful effort to that end in the lower courts, in which they were defeated by administration attorneys. Last week, however, the Supreme Court decided to hear an appeal on behalf of two British prisoners, two Australians, and the twelve Kuwaitis. The court will decide "whether the United States can set up prisons for foreigners outside of the court's scrutiny." The administration contends, and the lower courts agree, that the courts have no authority over the prisoners because Guantanamo is located in the territory of a sovereign foreign government. In a brief written by US Solicitor General Theodore B. Olson, the administration contends that any rights of these prisoners "are to be determined by the executive and the military, not the courts. The extraordinary circumstances implicate core political questions that the constitution leaves to the president as commander in chief."

The Kuwaiti families were said to be thrilled with the court's decision to hear their case, and expressed confidence that this will lead to the release of their sons. The odds, however, are not in their favor. To support their case in the past, the administration used arguments based on a 1944 case known as Korematsu v. United States. In its decision in that case, the court refused to intervene in the confinement in an internment camp of Fred Korematsu, a Japanese American citizen. In his writings, Chief Justice William Rehnquist has defended the court's reasoning in Korematsu (i.e., *inter arma silent leges*—"in times of war, the law is silent"). Moreover, this is the court that put George Bush in office. The Kuwaitis should keep the bubbly corked.

When a firm doing business in United States locates its headquarters in Barbados, it doesn't take a genius to recognize that they are doing this to circumvent U.S. laws. What they are doing may not be illegal, but it is dishonest. This is precisely what our president is doing by locating his non-POW camp in Cuba. The Supreme

Court may declare his action legal, but they cannot make it honest.

A man of good character is first and foremost an honest man. For an article in last Sunday's newspaper (Nov. 16, 2003), the *Los Angeles Times* interviewed voters in a suburb of St. Louis. They found that although these residents of the "show me" state may disagree with President Bush on many of his policies, almost all of them like him. They like him and will definitely vote for him, they say, because he is a man of good character.

The Shady Spot

The boy rattled the screen door a couple of times to shoo the flies away, then opened it just wide enough to slip through to the back porch. He wore the standard summer uniform for these parts: blue jeans, one leg rolled up to bicycle chain height, no shirt, and no shoes. The warm sun felt good on his back, but it was still early in the day, and he knew it would be hot and muggy before long.

The dog sidled up to him with a wagging tail and eyes looking for recognition. A quick rub behind the dog's ear was all the recognition he needed to come closer. The dog was your typical good-for-nothin' mutt, always making a nuisance of himself, tagging along everywhere you'd go. Wouldn't lay, wouldn't stay, wouldn't come, wouldn't bring in the cow for milking. If you threw a stick for him to fetch, he would chase after it like crazy, then flop down and chew on it for a while. Then he'd come running back without the stick, panting and wagging his tail to beg for another. The dog wasn't much to look at either. He had a long-haired light brown coat with white spots. He was a small dog that might have had some kind of spaniel in him, and maybe some shepherd.

Folks probably thought that was why they called him Shep. Truth is, the boy's mother had named him. There was this song "Old Shep"—a real tear jerker—that his uncle used to sing and play on the guitar. Every time the uncle picked up his guitar to play, it was a sure thing that before he put it down again, the boy's mother would ask him to sing "Old Shep" and it was a sure thing that she'd be shedding tears at the sad part. So the dog was named after the Shep in the song, but he sure didn't live up to his name. The Shep in the song jumped into a swimming hole to save his master from drowning, but this Shep was more likely to be the one to fall in and have to be pulled out by someone.

The boy yelled through the back door that he was going down to the Hanovers' place. The response from the kitchen included a stern warning to be home in time to get the chores done before supper. The boy put the dog in the barn and latched the door. Then he hopped on his bike and headed down the dirt road, ignoring the frantic barking from behind.

Their house sat atop the highest hill around. For bike riding, it was just the opposite of what you would want: downhill on the way out when you were fresh; uphill on the way home when you were tired. It was a square two story house with bare wood shingle siding that had turned black over the years. In front, there were three big pine trees that created a shady spot on the lawn where there was usually a nice breeze. It was one of the boy's favorite spots. It would have been a great place to take a nap with a straw hat over your face if the dog would ever leave you alone, which he wouldn't. Near the house was a windmill with a well house at its base. Downhill from there was an outhouse that still got used from time to time even though they now had a flush toilet inside the house. The small barn was a bit further on down.

The boy started out slowly, alternately coasting and braking his bike as he weaved his way down the hill. The first stretch was a narrow dirt road with deep ruts that made bike riding treacherous, but it soon fed into a wider gravel road. This wider road was a county road, which meant that a road grader would come along to grade it now and then. The county road had no ruts, but long before it was due to be graded, it would always have a washboard surface that was so rough it could shake your teeth out if they weren't fastened in real good. The old timers said the county road had once been a stage coach route. Down the road beyond the Hanover place there was a rundown three-story red brick house with maybe fifteen or twenty rooms and a long porch that wrapped almost all the way around it. This house, they said, had once been a hotel and stage-coach stop. Further on down the road was a public well with a hand pump, where folks could pump cool water into a tin cup tied to the pump.

* * *

The dog had been barking frantically for the best part of an hour when the boy's mother finally got around to looking into it. Well, it was no wonder the poor animal was barking. Who'd want to be locked up like this? She set the dog free and walked back up toward the house, shaking her head and mumbling to herself as she went.

The dog took off down the dirt road running hard like he knew exactly where he was going. It was hot, but he kept up a good pace by running fast for a while, slowing to a trot to catch his breath, and then picking up the pace again. When he spotted a couple of dogs playing in the road up ahead, he squeezed through the fence and picked up his run again in a cornfield along-side the road. It was late in the season and the corn was high. The corn rows were arrow-straight and spaced a couple of feet apart, with the lowest razor-sharp leaves mostly above the dog's height. That made it easy to run, but the air was dead still, which made the heat almost unbearable. The dog panted hard but kept on running.

* * *

When the boy rode up to their place, Bob and Luke Hanover were already talking about heading down to the swimming hole (seeing as how the day was a real scorcher). This swimming hole they were talking about was at a wide spot in Sugar Creek. The water in the swimming hole was a couple of feet over your head at its deepest point, and it was so full of catfish you could probably catch them by hand if you didn't value your hands too much. According to Bob and Luke's dad, the catfish kept the bottom dug out, and if there hadn't been any catfish, there wouldn't have been any swimming hole. The swimming hole was on Mary Dively's property. Kids around here had always climbed over Mary's pasture gate to get to it, and in the past, she had never seemed to mind, but lately she had been running them off.

But where there's a will, there's a way, and Bob and Luke Hanover had found a new way to get to the swimming hole that didn't take you anywhere near Mary Dively's pasture gate. Here's how it went: The interurban railway was an electric trolley line that ran between Peoria and Bloomington. The trolley cars were powered from an overhead cable. There were stops every few miles along the line where folks could get on and off. To reach the swimming hole by the new route, the boys would take a side road to an interurban crossing, where they would leave their bikes. Then they would walk along the tracks to a railroad trestle where the interurban passed over Sugar Creek. At the trestle, they would climb down the bank to the creek bed and follow the creek upstream to the swimming hole. Bob and Luke had already done this a couple of times, and insisted it was not much harder than going the old way.

With this as their plan, the three boys set off down the county road on their bikes. After about a half mile, they rounded the first big bend in the road, where the roadside hand pump, always a welcome sight on a hot day like today, came into view. But what the boy saw today was not a welcome sight, for standing there at the well was the good-for-nothin' dog, lapping up water from a puddle under the pump for all he was worth. When he saw the boy, the dog put his head down, put his tail between his legs, and slinked toward him, sort of wobbling back and forth and keeping his body so close to the ground his belly almost dragged. Well if this didn't top it all! The biggest problem was that the dog had no better sense than to bark at every other dog he saw, large or small, which got him into fights he couldn't finish and had to be rescued from. The boy reckoned he would have to deal with this at least a couple of times on the way home. He scolded the dog (for all the good that would do), and they all took a long drink from the well before they hit the road again—the boys on their bikes, and the dog running along at the side of the road, sniffing in the ditch on one side, then crossing over to sniff the other side, all while lifting his leg from time to time to leave his mark, which he somehow managed to do almost without stopping.

They followed the tracks to the creek and the creek to the swimming hole according to plan. But what they saw as they approached the swimming hole was not in their plan: there stood old Mary Dively beside her pickup truck, looking like a defiant Annie Oakley, hat shoved back on her head, feet spread out, and hands on her hips. Mary had planted herself squarely between the boys and the swimming hole, and she was not in a good mood. Before the boys had a chance to say a word, Mary lit into them. She ordered them in very colorful words to get off her property, and to stay off.

Walking back along the creek toward the interurban tracks, the boys discussed what they wished they had said to Mary Dively (instead of "yes ma'am"), and likely would say if they ever got another chance. By the time they got back to the interurban trestle, the sun was still fairly high in the sky, which meant they had some time to kill. The trestle was built on a heavy timber framework that rose up from the creek bed to the level of the rail grade. At the top of the framework, heavy stringers were laid lengthwise along the support frame from one creek bank to the other, and were nailed to it using huge spikes. Ties were nailed on top of the stringers with spikes, and rails were laid on the ties. This was called "open-deck construction" because it left open spaces between the ties. Most of whatever fell on the trestle (like sleet or snow) would fall through the spaces to the creek, some twenty odd feet below.

The timber framework presented a tempting challenge to the boys, who were soon proving their bravery by climbing all over it. The dog kept busy hunting for prey, real or imagined. He would sniff and run; then crouch, then pounce and growl viciously. Then he might look around to see if anyone had noticed before doing it again.

It took no time at all for the boys to learn that the timbers were coated with black and sticky creosote that came off the timbers real easy, but then stuck to the boys like glue. They tried to wash it off in the creek, but this futile effort soon gave way to wading and splashing each other. The water was plenty deep enough for wading, but sharp rocks in the creek bed took most of the fun out that. The boys needed to find something else to do.

Bob thought the interurban ought to be coming along soon. He knew from a cowboy movie he'd seen that you could tell when a train was coming by listening with your ear pressed against the track. To check this out, they climbed up the bank to the end of the trestle where the interurban would be starting across. To make it more interesting, they would put an ear to the rail, and when they heard the interurban coming would take off running to beat the car to the far end of the trestle.

They had no idea how much warning they would have, so they moved out to the middle of the trestle to give themselves a head start. Then they took some trial runs to see how fast they could run along the railroad ties without losing their footing. Their results convinced them to move the starting point even further toward the far end of the trestle. Now, at their new starting point they sat on the rails, talking and taking turns listening for the approaching interurban.

* * *

A few miles up the line, the interurban trolley was moving along at its normal running speed of 20 to 25 miles an hour. The driver sat at the front of the car where he had a good view of the tracks ahead. He kept his hand on the brass handle that controlled the car's speed. To the right of the speed handle was a pull-lever for the brakes, and overhead was a cord tied to a warning bell the driver rang at road crossings. It had been a pleasant ride so far, but now it was starting to get uncomfortably warm in the car. Passengers were opening windows, some of the men were fanning themselves and reading magazines and newspapers, and a few ladies patted at their faces with hankies and chatted as they watched the scenery go by.

* * *

Back at the trestle, the boys had been listening impatiently for a hum or whatever it was you were supposed to hear when a train was coming down the track. The warning came sooner than expected—but in the form of the familiar 'clang clang clang' of the interurban bell—and it sounded much too close.

For a brief moment, the boys sat there with their mouths open, exchanging startled looks. Then they jumped up and began a frantic run for their lives, glancing nervously at the creek below and screaming loudly as they went. Have you ever had one of those dreams where you want desperately to run but can hardly move your legs? Well, that was how the boys felt now as they struggled to run fast while avoiding the gaps between the ties.

The dog was still working back and forth along the creek bank when he heard the boys' terrified screams and saw them running across the trestle. Now, he wheeled and scrambled up the bank, following the route the boys had taken earlier. Dirt and rocks flew out behind him as he scratched for a hold. His paws were bleeding, the muscles in his shoulders and hips burned, and his heart pounded as never before.

Safely reaching the end of the trestle well ahead of the arrival of the interurban car, the boys stood for a moment gasping for breath. Then they hopped down the short distance to the bottom of the grade to wait for the interurban. Now, forgetting the terror that had gripped them just a short moment ago, they laughed and congratulated each other with slaps on the back and playful shoulder punches.

CLANG! CLANG! CLANG! The interurban was approaching fast. The boy looked up expecting to see the trolley car, but what immediately caught his eye was the dog, a few yards from the other end of the trestle. The dog was trying to run to him, but was stumbling with nearly every step as first one leg, then another slipped between the ties. The boy waved his arms and yelled as loud as he could: BACK SHEP! GO BACK!

Confused, the dog momentarily stopped and looked back, but then he continued to run toward the boy, even harder than before. The dog's eyes were fixed on the boy's with a look that urgently cried out to him for help. The interurban car now loomed huge behind the little dog, careening toward him at high speed. Looking first over his shoulder at the oncoming trolley car and then back at the boy, the dog ran even harder. As the boy stood there helpless to do anything, he could only watch the dog's rear end churning up and down behind his head as he tried to run toward him. The dog stumbled and fell, struggled to his feet again and ran, then stumbled again. When the trolley was just a few short yards away, the dog leaped for the side of the trestle in a desperate attempt to escape. When the trolley hit him, it pulled the dog under the carriage, where in slow motion, it bounced him about like a stuffed toy, and finally tossed him over the side to tumble over and over as he fell to the creek below.

The boy stood in stunned silence as the interurban continued on its way. After the car passed, he bounded over the track and clambered down the bank, slipping, rolling, and sliding to the creek bed below. The dog was on his back on the rocks with his entire head and upper half of his body submerged in the creek. Tears filled the boy's eyes as he picked up the limp, broken body. Gradually, the reality of the horror he had just witnessed, and his part in it, struck him like a blast of icy cold air, and he began to sob uncontrollably.

Bob and Luke, now at the boy's side, tried to console him, aware that they too shared responsibility. Thoughts of their daring race with death—a story that would surely have improved with each telling—had vanished. Their innocent afternoon of summer fun had lost its innocence. It now seemed that there was nothing they could do here to help—the boy himself had said as much—so they thought they'd better be getting on home.

Now, sitting alone beside the creek with the dog in his arms, the boy tried, through his sobs, to speak. Repeatedly, he told the dog how sorry he was. He went on at length, talking to a dog who could not hear his words, see his tears, or feel his arms.

Much later, as the sun began to sink behind the trees, the boy's crying softened, and finally, ended.

With great effort, he slowly managed to get to his feet and climb the steep bank to the tracks above, with the dog in his arms. Back at the road, he found his bicycle, gently laid the dog in a carrier basket over the front wheel, and started off for home. By the time he reached the dirt road, the sun was gone and the blue sky was growing dark. From here on, he would walk beside his bicycle as he pushed it up the hill.

* * *

The mother was busily cleaning up after supper, pausing every minute or so to look out through the kitchen window toward the Hanover place. All she could see was the Hanovers' pole light, and she was worried. The boy had never stayed out this late before. Something serious must have happened. Finally, in the darkness, she made out his thin dark figure, bending forward as he pressed against the handlebars of the bicycle.

She was out of breath when she reached him. She looked back and forth between the crumpled ball of fur in the basket and the boy, who would not allow his eyes to meet hers. This was not the time for explanations. Silently, they pushed the bicycle the rest of the way to the house, where they laid the dog in his favorite sleeping spot, under the windmill in a corner of the well house. Now, the mother took the boy in her arms and comforted him as only she could. Tomorrow, they would dig a grave in the front yard, in the shady spot under the pines.

Vi Hinton

I want my children, my grandchildren, even my great grandchildren to know that this aging woman they sometimes visit has not always been this aging woman. I want them to see that I was once a curious child, a vibrant young woman with dreams, a sometimes unsure wife and mother and a traveler to obscure parts of the world.

And so I write of my wild early childhood growing up in lumber camps, of the taming of the wild child in a one-room schoolhouse, and of the discipline that changed me from a timid fearful probie into a confident registered nurse. I write of serving in the Army Nurse Corps during World War II, of my children's unorthodox rearing while we lived in Southeast Asia, and of my sometimes bizarre adventures as I explored the less traveled areas of the globe.

"VJ Day in Aruba" is an account of some of my experiences as a young army nurse stationed on that island during World War II. The transformation of Aruba into a tourist destination could not have been imagined by any of us assigned to that tiny island during World War II. Now, high-rise luxury hotels dot the landscape. Except for the Dutch oil company expatriate community and the military base which were equipped with electricity, running water and flush toilets, we could have felt that we had landed on another planet, so alien the island seemed.

173

VJ Day in Aruba

Chickens squawked and ran for cover, pigs squealed in terror, dogs barked in alarm, cats, backs arched, climbed the nearest tree as the jeep careened wildly over the narrow, winding, pot-holed excuse for a road. The jeep, driven by a young officer who had celebrated too long at the local bar before making the rounds of the military base to pick up two fellow officers and a young, newly commissioned army nurse, sped through the small village and into the country-side, not once but repeatedly. The occupants of the vehicle, boisterous, singing and laughing with unrestrained mirth, had just heard the news that the war was over. They would be going home! Some men had been stationed for two and a half years on Aruba, that seven and a half by three and three quarters miles spit of land in the Caribbean Sea.

I was a young nurse aboard the weaving, speeding jeep. Although I had been on that small island only a few months, I was already feeling an almost claustrophobic sense of being confined in a too small space. I could only imagine the tedium and the sense of isolation my fellow passengers had experienced during their sojourn on that tiny piece of land. Aruba was not only infinitesimally small in the vast expanse of the Caribbean (in my half-sleep I sometimes imagined it, and all of us on its soil, being totally engulfed by a tidal wave) it was desert-like and nearly flat. Aside from the assorted cacti that flourished profusely, the distinguishing features were the Divi-Divi trees, which grew straight to roughly three feet and thereafter were forced into a horizontal position by the incessant strong dry winds endemic to the region. The only relief from those dust-blowing winds came with the rain-laden winds during only two months of the year. It was during those two months that all the fresh water available for the year was collected in cisterns at the base of corrugated metal stretched along the hillsides. From a distance the hillsides gave the impression of giant wash boards laid side by side.

The ever-present cacti served the native population in a variety of ways. Our wash women used them as clothes lines for drying our laundry, necessitating close examination of each piece of clothing before dressing.

However, checking for thorns paled in significance when compared with a far greater hazard. Scorpions, their bite potentially deadly if on the neck or near the heart area, often lurked in the folds of garments, inside shoes or in bedding. As a result we developed both morning and nightly rituals. In the morning we shook out every item of clothing we planned to wear that day, turning each piece inside out searching for any elusive stowaways. Shoes, too, had to be shaken and visually examined to prevent the possibility of a painful sting. At night we carefully inspected all bed coverings, pillows and sleepwear for the unwelcome creatures.

We encountered another unsavory life form on a daily basis: giant centipedes that made their home in our shower. The shower, attached to the tiny cottage I shared with one other nurse at our small field hospital, was a roofless sort of lean-to. The dirt floor, covered by a slatted wooden platform, absorbed the sun-heated water suspended in a large canister overhead and activated by a rope pulley. High barbed wire fence surrounding our cottage discouraged would-be Peeping Toms.

There were fun things to do. One was the daily late afternoon volleyball game with the hospital staff. The corpsmen seemed to take inordinate pleasure in seeing their ward nurse out of uniform and wearing shorts. They may not have been aware that their on-duty supervisor rather enjoyed eyeing her male counterparts in brief garb, as well.

Aruba's swimming beaches were unsurpassed, covered with pinkish white sand, and reached only after gingerly stepping over and around a carpet of large, perfectly shaped conch shells, each one more spectacular than the last and each inviting closer inspection. Often the temperature of the crystal blue transparent water, soothing and hypnotic, tempted me to float in a dream-like trance only to become aware that I had been carried by the tide farther from shore than was safe. Frantically, then, I would swim back to shore pledging to be more careful next time. On more energetic days I, with my swimming companions, explored sunken German war ships sent to watery graves early in war as they attempted to sabotage the oil refineries, which dominated that Dutch territory in the West Indies.

Occasionally, residents of the refinery community invited the two military doctors and one or both of the nurses for dinner or a game of dominoes, played with beautiful ivory tiles. It was at one of those dinners that

VJ Day in Aruba

I was introduced to the very strong, almost thick demi-tasse coffee dear to the heart of the Dutch.

As we circled the island celebrating the occasion of that memorable day, later to be known as V-J day, I reminisced on my introduction to the Dutch military base hosting some five thousand American troops. As I alighted from the plane that brought me there from Puerto Rico, I noticed a long line of GIs at the arrival gate. Later I learned that the refrain, "She's young! She's young!" was passed along the line. I was replacing a forty-year old who, to an eighteen or nineteen year-old recruit, seemed next to ancient, I suppose. Being one of only two women on the base, I was a bit of a novelty.

I remembered, too, the succession of foreign merchant seamen dropped off at our hospital when their ship docked for refueling at the refinery. Two, in particular, stood out in my memory: one, a Swedish sailor with a fractured femur, spoke no English (our staff spoke no Swedish). I remembered his look of absolute euphoria when a beautiful blond Swedish woman, who was part of a USO troupe that had come to entertain our servicemen sat at his bedside holding his hand and speaking to him in his native tongue. His face was aglow, a picture of pure ecstasy.

An even more memorable experience had to do with an off-loaded sailor with a hot appendix. His grave condition precluded sending him on to Puerto Rico for surgery. Our small ill-equipped operating room was inadequate for performing major surgery; however, necessity being the mother of invention, the doctor who was not a surgeon and a nurse who was not an operating room nurse, proceeded to remove the inflamed appendix. The patient's scar may have been a bit wavy but we saved his life and sent him to recuperate at the large military hospital in Puerto Rico.

I remember, too, the moonlight swims in the velvety smooth still water of the lagoon; the breathtaking radiant sunsets at exactly 6 o'clock each evening abruptly followed by intense darkness; the long serious conversations with the base chaplain about the meaning of life and love as we sat on the steps of the nurse's cottage.

As we celebrated the end of hostilities and the prospect of going home, I was happy to anticipate leaving the confines of that dusty, dry, hot slice of land in the sea. I could empathize with the young men who had felt imprisoned there for too long. But a part of Aruba would remain in my thoughts and heart for a lifetime.

Mary Jenkins

My name is Mary Louise Dickson Jenkins. I am the eighth of ten children born to Warren Earl Dickson and Margaret Alma Igou Dickson. We were born and raised in a small town, Tyrone, Pennsylvania. My father was born in 1903, died in 1994; my mother was born in 1904, died in 1989. They lived through most of the twentieth century and witnessed or were part of the many changes that took place throughout that century. My mother once made the statement, with wonder in her voice, "I have lived from the days of the horse and buggy to seeing man walk on the moon." Over the years, at family get-to-gathers, we have talked about growing up with fond memories, and there was always much laughter. My mother was an ordinary woman of her day with what I term an extraordinary attitude, faith and love. She had her trials and tribulations, but nothing that could keep her down. She is the person I admire most. I feel that her descendants would enjoy and should know the family story and so decided to write a book. I will probably title the book either "Margaret's Triumphs" or "The Dickson Saga."

The following excerpt starts in the fall of 1931, a year after the birth of my brother, Dick, their seventh child, and three years before my birth. At the time we were living a few miles south of Tyrone, which had no hospital and about seven miles from Altoona where the nearest hospital was located.

These were the years of the "great depression."

1931–1932

The year following Dick's birth, Mom was house cleaning, preparing for the Thanksgiving holiday. There was a window in the attic. There was no floor in the attic, but a window was there and Mom was determined to wash it. Carrying the cleaning paraphernalia and carefully making her way, she fell between two joists, falling through the ceiling over the stairway. As she landed on her back, her right ankle collided with one of the steps so hard that the foot was lying beside her leg, connected only by a small amount of tissue and a flap of skin.

Someone called the doctor, and when he got there he put numerous tourniquets on her leg. He explained to the neighbors that shock and the force of the blow her leg took when hitting the step had collapsed the veins and arteries, sending the blood back toward the heart. That condition wouldn't last long, and when it let go, the tourniquets wouldn't stop her from bleeding to death. Saying Mom couldn't wait for an ambulance, he had the neighbors help him put Mom on the back seat of his car, and he drove as fast as possible to the Altoona hospital. Mom prayed they could save her foot.

When Mom reached the hospital the surgeons took her immediately into surgery and did their best to reattach her foot. There was no time to clean her, other than the immediate area they were operating on. Mom survived, but as the weeks passed, her foot and ankle turned blacker and blacker. Her fever was high and oftentimes she was delirious. On the afternoon of December 24th, fearing to delay any longer, the doctors told her that they would have to amputate her leg to the knee in the morning.

By this time the doctors had nurses sitting at Mom's bedside around the clock. Sometime during the night Mom woke up. She looked at the nurse and said, "Its okay. They don't have to take the leg off." The nurse, thinking Mom was delirious, and wanting to humor her said, "Yes, yes dear. You'll be okay." She wiped Mom's brow and took her temperature. She was surprised to see the temperature was normal, so she took it again. As the nurse charted the first normal temperature since Mom was admitted, Mom fell into a peaceful sleep.

Six am, Christmas morning, the doctors came in, talked to the nurse and read Mom's chart. While they were reading the chart, Mom woke up and calmly said, "Its okay. You don't have to take the leg off." She stated this so simply and with such assurance that the doctors reexamined the foot and took her temperature again. It was still normal. Finally, one of the doctors said, "The foot is still black, doesn't look any different, but I get the feeling that something is going on here. We'll wait a little longer and see what happens."

Mom spent many months flat on her back, her leg in traction immobilizing her foot. Gradually, she improved although the ankle still festered. The doctor was going to send for leeches to put in the wound, but her attending physician, Dr. Gilbraith, remembered reading something in one of his father's old charts of a wound healed by applying the sap of a pine tree for a period of time. He collected some pine sap from a tree in his yard and applied it to Mom's wound and left it bandaged for a week. He found it was considerably improved, so repeated the pine sap dressing for another week and the wound healed.

Mother had received a Christmas miracle. It would be fifteen years before she would learn the full extent of that miracle.

It was this Christmas that Mom told me about when dad went into the woods and cut down a little pine tree and put it up Christmas Eve after the kids were asleep. He decorated it with cotton he'd been collecting for some time from bottles of pills. Dad had walked into town and got an apple crate from behind a grocery store. He carefully took it apart, pounded the nails straight and reassembled it into a sled which was the present that the kids shared on Christmas day.

When Dad went to visit Mom in the hospital on Christmas afternoon, Mom asked him what they'd had for dinner. Dad told her they'd had a can of baked beans and some potatoes. Sitting on her bedside table was a nice basket of fruit that dad's parents had brought her when they'd visited earlier. Mom told dad to take it home to the kids. He didn't want to take it from her but she insisted, saying that she had plenty to eat in the hospital, and she wouldn't be able to eat a bite of that fruit, knowing the kids had little to nothing to eat. Dad took it home to the kids, who didn't waste a minute digging into it.

After spending many months in the hospital, Mom was finally allowed to come home. For several more months she was pretty much confined to bed. Paul, who was nine years old at the time, did the cooking under Mom's instruction. When the baby needed his diaper changed, Paul would carry him in and lay him on the bed next to Mom and she would take care of him. Neighbors helped out from time to time but Mom tried not to be a burden to them. She believed a family should do whatever and as much as it could for itself.

Before long she was able to use crutches to get around. Within days she discovered that a chair was far more useful than crutches. Mom found that she could put her knee on a chair and scoot around the house. With her knee supported on the chair, both hands were free to do dishes or the laundry. If she got tired she could sit down and peel potatoes for dinner or iron clothes. Even when she was outside, the chair was handier than the crutches. With her knee balanced on the chair, she could hang clothes on the line. She could pump water into the bucket to take into the house, and if she got tired while only half way across the yard, she could stop and sit for a while.

Her young sons helped out when necessary and with whatever they were capable of doing, but Mom was determined not to take the childhood from them that she, herself, had never had. And if you're wondering where Dad was during this time, he was out looking for any work he could get. These were the years of the Great Depression.

Eventually she was able to walk, though she would always limp. One day while at the doctor's office, he asked the nurse to bring in Mom's x-rays. Mom told him they never took any x-rays, there wasn't time. He told her with an injury as bad as hers there had to be x-rays. After a thorough search and a call to the hospital, he discovered she was right. He had some x-rays taken of Mom's ankle, and, after checking them, he asked her how she had gotten to his office. She told him she had taken the bus. He asked Mom how she had gotten from the bus stop to his office. She told him she had walked. He asked her to walk around his office, which she did. He told her, "I don't know what's holding you up, but it won't hold you up for long."

He showed Mom the x-rays. There was no ankle bone; in fact there was no bone between her foot and her leg. He scheduled her for surgery and when the time came, he got a pig's knuckle from the butcher and sterilized it to be used as an ankle bone for her. It served her well. After the surgery, Mom was able to move her foot up and down, though she was never able to move it side to side.

1932–1935

It was about this time, 1932, two families moved in with us, the Consentinos and the Hausers, who were a help to Mom, great friends and good company. By now, none of them could afford to pay rent, but the farmer who owned the house realized he couldn't rent it to anybody else, so he let them stay there because he knew they would take care of it and keep the hobos from moving in. There was a railroad nearby.

One day Mom was sitting on the porch watching Dick, who was playing in the yard, when she and Dick spotted a snake at the same time. Like any two-year-old, Dick went after the snake. Mom couldn't run, but she was screaming, and moving as fast as she could to get to the baby when Don Halbritter, who heard her screams, came running. He grabbed the baby and handed him to her then went back and picked up the snake and held it up for Mom to see. It was a big black snake and harmless. Mom was still shaking, so he got rid of it in the woods.

The men spent their days looking for work or gleaning the potato fields and apple orchards for the leftovers after the harvests. They also went hunting for deer, rabbit, and squirrel, occasionally, out of season. When your families are hungry you just do what you have to do. The women cooked and canned whatever was brought home. They got more apples than anything else so there was plenty of apple butter. The boys took apple butter sandwiches to school, for lunch every day. That's all they had. [My brother] June is seventy-five-years old, now, and has not touched apple butter since the mid-1930s.

Dad often walked five to ten miles looking for work. Sometimes he would get hired on for just one day, and he never turned the job down. One day's wages were better than none at all. Sometimes he'd be hired on for a couple weeks, and if it was miles from home the family only saw him on weekends. There was no shame in being jobless because so many others were in the same predicament. Mom used to say, "There's no shame in being poor, but there's no excuse for being dirty." If she had no soap she'd boil the clothes till all the dirt came out.

Mom told me of one winter when it was very cold, Dad and Joe hitchhiked to the welfare office in Altoona to ask for coal. He explained that we were out and the kids were cold. They told him his name would go on the list and he should get some coal in about a week. Dad was never one for arguing; he simply got up, said "Come on, Joe. Let's go home and start burning the furniture." Evidently they could see he meant it because by the time Dad and Joe had walked and hitchhiked home, there was a truck there unloading the coal. Dad spoke quietly and never minced words, and he always meant what he said. Dad never made a promise he didn't keep.

Winters were hard on everyone; still kids would find ways to have fun: sledding down hill on a piece of cardboard, snowball fights, and sliding on the ice on a frozen stream. The hardest part was wearing shoes, mostly someone's hand-me-downs. You were lucky if they were a little too big. You could put cardboard in them to cover the holes in the soles and for extra insulation. Maybe even room for an extra pair of socks if you had them.

The worst was when the sole was coming loose from the shoe. You could put a rubber jar band (used in canning) around the shoe to hold it on but that wouldn't last long. Mostly you just "goose stepped" around school. It was the depression era, and a lot of kids were in the same "boat" and "goose stepping" right along with you, everybody lifting the knee high and coming down quick to make sure the sole landed flat on the ground. It was the "pits" when you miscalculated and bent the sole back.

Mom told me that she had two wishes through these years. One was that she could buy all the kids new shoes at the same time to start school; the other was that she could get cocoa and sugar at the same time so she could make the kids a cup of hot cocoa before she put them to bed. Occasionally she had cocoa and sometimes she had sugar but she rarely had both at the same time. I don't ever remember Mom saying she wanted anything for herself.

Summer was better—no school, exploring the fields and hills, wading in the small streams, swimming in the deeper ponds and best of all no shoes.

In the evenings, after the kids went to bed, the adults played cards. I remember Mom telling me that they wore the spots off the cards. They couldn't afford a new deck, but somebody found a crayon and they drew the spots back on whenever needed. They talked and laughed a lot during those times. Mom said, "It was laugh or go crazy in those days," and she couldn't afford to go crazy. Crazy was a luxury.

One day Dot Hauser and Mary Cosentino, noticing that they'd washed the paint off the walls while trying to keep the house clean, went into town and went to all the paint stores, hardware stores, and decorating stores, asking for old, outdated wallpaper sample books. They brought them home and started matching colors and designs. The floral wallpaper went into the living room, striped wallpaper in the dining room and checked and plaid wallpaper in the kitchen.

Welfare had given them a one-hundred-pound sack of flour to make bread. Mom mixed some of the flour with water to make paste. Since her leg still bothered her, her job was to sit at the kitchen table and paste the wallpaper, which Dot and Mary then applied to the room for which it was intended. When the job was done they declared it colorful, cheerful, and clean. (I think that may have been the forerunner of the psychedelic era.)

Although welfare gave us one hundred-pound sacks of flour and potatoes, they never gave any yeast. Often, Mom would have to ask Dad's brother, Uncle Fred, for three cents to buy some yeast so she could bake bread. Welfare didn't give money in those days; in fact it was more like today's food banks. As bad as things were, Mom always said we were fortunate because we lived in the country where neighbors let us keep whatever leftovers we could find after the harvest. The boys usually found potatoes and corn that Mom made stretch through the winter, and there was an abundance of apples that Mom made into applesauce and apple butter, which she canned. In the fall the men could go hunting to put some meat on the table. Mom said she didn't know how the city folk survived.

There was a neighbor who had some cows. He once mentioned that one of his cows had quit giving milk. Mom said little did he know that that cow was putting out a lot more milk than his other cows. Every kid in the neighborhood was milking it. It was the only one in the field that would stand still so they were all taking milk from the same cow.

On Sept 21, 1934, Mary Louise Dickson (me) was born in that house at Fouss's Mill. I was the eighth child, and second daughter.

Although the three families only lived together until the spring of 1935 (by then the men had found work and each moved his family into a home of his own), they remained good friends for the rest of their lives.

1935–1937

In early March 1935, Dad moved the family to 1208 Washington Avenue. That was only six blocks from Grandma's house. This house had running water and a bathroom. The big drawback was the railroad tracks were about eighteen feet from the front door. But that was also a plus in the winter time because it provided free coal. As the train slowly moved down the tracks, the boys would jump on board and roll off big lumps of coal which were hauled into the cellar. They never told Mom.

Now that we were living in Tyrone, the boys no longer had to go on the bus to Bellwood; they walked to Logan school a couple blocks away. Paul, Huff, and June were each put back one year in school. June particularly hated this because it put him in the same class with his brother, Don, who was a year younger. June hated school and played hooky most days it snowed, to earn money shoveling it from people's sidewalks. He always gave the money to Mom to help out with the bills.

One day Huffy heard Mom say she wished she had a nice blanket to wrap the baby in so she could take her to see Grandma. It snowed that night. The next day Huffy, 11 years old, played hooky from school and went out shoveling snow from sidewalks all day. He went to the 5 and 10 cent store with the money he earned and bought a new baby blanket and a dress for the baby, took them home, handed them to Mom and said, "Here, take baby Mary over to see Grandma." Mom was overwhelmed with pride and gratitude. How do you punish sons like that for playing hooky?

Carol Arlene Dickson, the ninth child and third daughter, was born in that house on Sept 27, 1935. This was not an easy birth. Mom said when labor began the bed had to be prepared. In those days, when having the baby at home, you sewed a four-foot square muslin "envelope," leaving one end open in order to stuff it with crumpled newspapers to absorb the water and blood so the mattress wouldn't be ruined. Afterward, it was taken out and burned. Mom had done this when giving birth to all of us, except Dick, who was born in the Phillipsburg Hospital.

Mom had made up the bed, placed the "envelope," and went to the bathroom to bathe, before sending for the doctor. While in the bathroom she started hemorrhaging. She heard Paul come in from school and yelled down for him to go to the neighbor's and tell them to call the doctor to come right away. Then he was to wait for the other kids to come home from school and take them next door; they were not to come up stairs for any reason.

Mom didn't want the kids to see the blood. She had left a trail from the bathroom to the bedroom. She'd lost a lot of blood and was too weak to get into the bed. When the doctor arrived, he found her on her knees with the top half of her on the bed. That was as far as she could make it. Dad came rushing in right after the doctor had arrived, and together they got her on to the bed. The placenta was being expelled and the baby had not yet been delivered.

The doctor worked fast and managed to save both Mom and the baby. Mom said Carol didn't cry like any other newborn; she sobbed like her little heart was broken. While the doctor was delivering the baby, the neighbor cleaned up the blood in the bathroom and hallway so the kids wouldn't see it and be frightened.

It was customary to stay in bed for ten days after giving birth. This time Mom really didn't have a choice because she was so weak from the blood loss. Friends looked after the kids and took care of Mom and the babies. Mary and Carol were just a year and six days apart in age.

Huff tells of the time when the boys got a dog. I believe it was while we were living in this house. Dad finally was working, so he let them keep the dog that followed Paul home. Weeks later the kids came running in saying that the dog catcher had just caught the dog. Dad stormed out of the house and grabbed the dog out of the dog catcher's arms saying, "Gawd-dammit! Can't these kids have anything?" The dog catcher didn't utter a word. He just got in his truck and drove away. It's the only time Huff can remember ever hearing Dad swear.

One day that summer June asked a friend if he could have a ride on his bicycle. Don got on the handlebars, and off they went. But they didn't go around the block; instead they rode down to the stone quarry at Ironsville, a couple miles out of town. When June and Don didn't come right back, the friend went to the grocery store where Dad worked and told him they had stolen his bike. On their way home, a car came out of a side street and hit them. June saw it coming in time to lift his leg over the crossbar and that probably saved him from a broken leg. When the car hit them dead-center Don went straight up in the air and landed on his feet when he came down. The bike and June went side ways and June was scratched up a bit but not seriously hurt.

The man put both boys in the car and the bike in the trunk and drove them to the doctor's office. While the doctor was examining June and washing his scratches, Don, who was sitting in the waiting room, decided he wasn't hurt and got up and went home. Dad was there, having lunch, and he gave Don a good spanking with the belt for stealing the bike. He promised June would get a spanking, too, as soon as he got his hands on him. Dad and Mom had not heard about the accident yet. Dad went back to work, and later that afternoon Dr.

Murchinson knocked on Mom's door asking if Don was home. Mom told him he was in bed being punished, and the doctor asked if he could examine him. He told Mom about the accident and that June was okay. He said dad shouldn't have spanked Don because for all anyone knew he might have internal injuries. Mom, worried, hurried the doctor to the bedroom where he checked Don and said he was okay.

(Carol, who is a retired nurse, says this "boggles her mind." Nowadays, no one would dare take someone else's kid to a doctor, nor would a doctor treat them without a parent's consent. And certainly no doctor, today, would go to someone's house looking for him after he'd walked out of his waiting room.)

The Noel's lived next door. One day Mom heard Mrs. Noel screaming that her baby wasn't breathing. Mom hurried over there and held the baby upside down and shook him, pounded on his back and blew air into his mouth. In the meantime, one of the kids went running for the doctor. The baby coughed up some phlegm and started to gasp for air just before the doctor got there. The doctor said the baby had whooping cough and he bawled Mom out for being there. He said, "With all those kids you have, do you want to take the whooping cough home to them?" Mom could never have ignored a sick baby and besides, she wasn't thinking; she was reacting to a need. The Good Lord watched over us. Mrs. Noel's baby lived, and none of us got the whooping cough.

1937–1940

In 1937 we moved to 1561 Pennsylvania Avenue, one block from the paper mill. It was four blocks from the grocery store where dad worked. This house had no bathroom, but there was a toilet at the end of the hallway, upstairs. No door, no curtain, no privacy. Nearly every time someone started upstairs you'd hear a yell, "I'm up here." meaning I'm on the toilet; wait.

On Sept 6, 1937, Robert Bruce Dickson (Bob) was born. He was the tenth child and seventh son. After the doctor had delivered the baby, the nurse took Bob down to the kitchen to bathe him. As the community nurse, Betty Close, was bathing the baby, eight-year-old Pat came into the kitchen and said, "Oh, a baby! He's cute. Whose is he?" The nurse said, "He's your new little brother." And Pat said, "Oh no, he can't be ours. We have too many kids already. If you leave him here, Daddy will be mad." Mrs. Close told the doctor that was one of the funniest things she'd ever heard.

Bob was born on Labor Day, which seems appropriate. The older boys were at the auto race track, near Tipton, watching the car races. The doctor arrived before the boys left for the races, and he sat in the rocking chair while Mom packed lunches for the boys to take with them. She wanted them out of the house for the day. They wanted to know what the doctor was doing there, and Mom told them he'd just come to visit. She assured them no one was sick. Like Pat, when they got home they were surprised to find a new baby brother.

It was always a surprise when a new baby showed up. (I recently asked Don where he thought babies came from when he was a little boy, and he told me he thought they came in the doctor's little black bag.) Mom did not believe pregnancy was something children needed to know about. Mom had always been heavy, so her pregnancies didn't show. I once asked Dad if Mom had ever been slim, like maybe in high school. He said no, that she'd always been heavy and she was a beautiful young lady.

It was the first Christmas in this house that dad went out and bought Mom a radio on credit the day before Christmas. He brought it home at noon, plugged it in, and turned it on. He went back to work and Mom listened and sang to music all day and all evening while she got the house ready for Christmas day. The day after Christmas, he unplugged the radio and returned it to the store. He told them he really couldn't afford it. When Mom asked him why he did that to begin with, he told her he couldn't afford to buy her a present, but the very least she deserved was to listen to her beloved music, if only for a day. When Mom told me about this, years later, she said she could still hear the music and felt blessed that dad cared enough to do that for her. He had a lot of pride and must have hated returning that radio to the store even though he never intended to keep it for more than that one day.

One Saturday that following summer Mom and a neighbor, Ruth Phillips, went to the movies. During the movie Mom was feeling pressure and went to the restroom. Mom had a miscarriage. She got Ruth and they went home. That was Mom's eleventh and last pregnancy. She'd had ten children in fourteen years. Mom continued to bleed over the next couple months and she was having some pain. The doctor finally convinced Mom to go to the hospital and have a hysterectomy. The boys were in their early teens and capable of caring for themselves while Mom was in the hospital. Mom's friend, Ruth, took Carol, Bob and me to stay with her till Mom came home and things got back to normal.

Paul Sammy Larkin

My autobiographical writings start in Springfield, MO on January of 1932. From Missouri, in the summer of 1940 our family; Father, Mother, and 5 children moved to a small village in Mississippi. From there my parents sent us children, now three girls and three boys, away to Catholic schools for our education in several states: Missouri, Arkansas, Louisiana and Alabama.

These writings tell the story of my Larkin family and their journey and struggles for education and growth in a sometimes alien southern world in those tumultuous 1930 Depression years, the 1940 WW II years, and the challenging 1950s.

My motivation for this exercise is to preserve certain 'moments in time' of a family, for posterity.

The Transition—Summer 1940— Springfield, MO, to Amory, MS

My third year in grammar school was coming to an end, and not too soon! Summer Freedom!

Mother was hinting that something big was coming for the whole family. It finally began to sink in that when school was out, we all were moving from our big two-story home in Springfield, MO, to somewhere far, far to the south, where Dad was being transferred in his job as pipe-fitter and sheet-metal worker for the Frisco railroad.

The name given for the place in Dixie Land, 375 miles away to the southeast, was Amory, Mississippi. I envisioned mystery, excitement—always warm weather, bare feet, sunshine—but what I didn't yet know: sweltering, withering, humid, unrelenting night-and-day heat, with humidity to make one breathless; then add mosquitoes, red bugs, stinging ants, stinging flies, wasps, ticks, and a plethora of other irritating insects. In winter: cold dampness that insidiously penetrated through all layers of clothing—to the bone. Thank goodness I knew nothing of all this then, nor would it have changed anything anyway.

All was excitement and aflurry as we packed and readied ourselves for that trip to the train station and this incredible new family adventure. Frisco trains in 1940, as WW II loomed ominously on the edge of our continent and consciousness, were anything but as comfortable and commodious as trains today, but we thought it was the "cat's pajamas" at that time.

As our little Larkin troop mounted the steep metal steps to the sitting car, we began to learn railroad-car protocol. Dad and Mother sat with Carol Jane, the infant, on one side of the isle, while Mary Ann and we three boys sat on the other in convenient controlling eyesight of our parents. We sat with spacious double seats facing each other for convenience, with luggage and packages stowed in racks above and in space below the seats. Now we were ready to be off, for our first ride on the rails.

I thought that train would never get under way, but then with one sharp and several gentle lurches, we were finally moving and building speed as we clicked and clacked and bounced over those steel rails. The initial view we got out the window was the bleak, dark back side of the city, but eventually that train broke out to the open farm and wooded countryside, and we were on our way to new worlds to conquer.

I soon found out that on that shaking, rocking railroad car, among the normal conveniences of a small washroom for relieving one's self, we had a porter pushing a cart through the aisles with items such as hot coffee and cold drinks, sandwiches, candy, etc. There was a special car, designated as the dining car, where you could sit at an elegant table with cloth, silver, and crystal and have a fine meal and excellent drinks. Further there was a sleeping car, called a "Pullman," with small sitting rooms together with comfortable sleeping accommodations. Here were practically all the comforts of home—away from home. One could actually travel in relative luxury with a lounging room and a wet bar. All these our parents made us children aware of.

As we approached West Memphis, then a squat, shabby town on the Arkansas or west side of the "Great Muddy," our coal-burning steam engine began to throttle back in preparation for its slow crawl as it crossed the mighty iron span that bound the Eastern and Western lands of our nation. Now we crossed this wide water barrier, the "Ol' Man River," from *Show Boat*, the 1936 Kern-Hammerstein musical.

I asked Daddy; "Why are we moving so slow?" His rejoinder was, "This ponderously heavy locomotive pulling its following burden of passenger and freight cars shakes the bridge, and this slower speed puts less stress on the sustaining structure, damaging it less and thus giving it a longer life." It was an awesome trip across the widest north-south river in the U.S. with its endless whirlpools, each of which might easily have swallowed a large house. We children could not have conceived of such a vast amount of soil-clogged water massively moving beneath us. This truly was an unforgettable experience, though we did feel relief when it was over, and we reached the shore and Memphis.

Our Conductor in his smart dark blue uniform and shiny gold buttons, though all business, was also courteous and even friendly as he clipped our passes and got to know his passengers. He knew our dad and what his business was and made several extra visits back to see that we were settled and comfortable and if we needed anything.

From Memphis we now moved along the last 120 miles of track through small towns nestled in flat fields of corn and cotton and mixed hardwood and piney woods to our new life of discovery in the storied Dixieland south. What a life-changing and challenging adventure we were plunging into and how eager we were to know whatever Amory had to offer. The fates were yet to offer us overwhelming much for our growth and maturity in this new environment and it was best we knew nothing of what they held in store for us. Only in slow increments were we to gain this fresh knowledge, and mercifully this was surely best for us.

We children, having never traveled, especially on such a long and all important journey, were full of questions: "Where are we now?" "When will we cross the Mississippi?" "How wide is it?" "Is Memphis a big city?" "How long before we get to Amory?" "How big is this town?" "How long before we get there?" Our Parents needed the Patience of Job to put up with this fidgety, excited, wild bunch, and to control and to keep us busy and out of trouble must have been ever challenging.

We must have left Springfield on a very early morning train so as to arrive in Amory before dark on that glorious summer evening. Our journey of 475 miles over clickity-clackity rails and ties with whistles and jerks, slowing and starting, was finally at an end as we practically leapt from that magic metal carpet that dumped us into our new reality. Our family of seven must have been quite a sight, stepping down to the brick walkway, loaded down with suitcases, bags, boxes and all our stuff, relieved that we had finally arrived.

Reflecting on this major family move, I realize how this transition must have been tremendously difficult for our Parents. My Father was moving away from much of his family and many of his friends and his work and all his lifetime of experience in Springfield. It was perhaps even more painful for Mother, who also was leaving Father and Mother, sisters and brothers and their families as well as her coterie of lady friends who seemed more numerous than Macy's has customers. How could this most social of women leave all this and the town in which she grew up and treasured for a place she knew nothing about and not a soul, hidden in the piney woods of the Rebel South?

Just wait till Mary Larkin got down there and found out what these fine southerners with their vaunted hospitality had in store for her. Time would tell that she was actually much braver than she knew. Besides her strong Catholic Faith, and all that meant to her, her greatest strength would always be her adoring, loyal, hard working Husband. There was also that maternal love for her brood of two daughters and three little sons whose care and nurture must ever have impelled her forward. As this story might show, with perhaps some stops and starts along the way, Mary Larkin managed nobly.

Larkins' First Rental Home In Amory

After a few days in a boarding house, our family climbed into a taxi, that early afternoon in the middle of June 1940, for a rather short ride to an old well-structured Victorian one-story home on the southwest corner of First Avenue and Fifth Street. This house had been built before the Civil War. In fact, on the alley to the rear still remained a long low wooden row of 6 or 7 small connected rooms that had formerly housed slaves before the end of that conflict. We were only four blocks east of Main Street, where in the middle of the intersection stood a square pillar about ten feet high topped by a fine bronze statue of a young Confederate soldier armed with his long rifle and standing by his plow. The Civil War was always thus kept foremost in the minds of the Rebel town.

One of the first tasks our Mother set herself to after settling in was to attempt to contact the scattered handful of Catholics reported to live in town and become a part of this fledgling community. Early on we met one Catholic, Mrs. Butler. This somewhat severe elderly lady was to be a fixture in our young lives, for she not only babysat us occasionally but it was she who, on Saturdays, was deputed to attempt to teach us three Larkin boys our Catholic Catechism. What a thankless task that must have been.

One day shortly after moving in when Mrs. Butler was watching over us boys, ages eight, seven, and six respectively, we decided to be as realistic as possible in playing Indians in our backyard. The tiny slave quarters became our teepees as we danced about our Indian blanket with its multi colored designs, shouting, war whooping and shooting suction-cupped tipped arrows at each other. We, in our realistic raiment, had fashioned small patches of cloth tied by a cord at the waist, and other than some colorful paint and mud streaks on our faces and bodies, we wore nothing. This was liberating, authentic and accurately depicting, we thought, Indian boys down through the ages. Our racket must have brought Mrs. Butler huffing out to quell our boisterous enthusiasm.

She was scandalized to find practically naked little white boys recreating wild Indian dances and battles in the backyard. We found nothing wrong with our innocent games and were surprised at her red-faced, shocked reaction, forcing us into the house and into "proper" clothing. When Mom came home and all was related, she acted with shocked amazement, yet I suspect she was secretly mightily amused. Dad, on arriving home that evening, thought it was funny, chiding us lightly and requesting that we, when outside, wear a bit more modest raiment in the future. This story made its rounds in the neighborhood, being retold repeatedly with the result (is it any wonder?) that we three were immediately branded as wild boys.

Our next escapade I conceived of was my jumping off the garage roof. This tiny, one-car detached structure was hardly more than a tool shed off the back side of the house. With a towel, my necessary flying cape, tied securely around my neck, up to the sagging roof I carefully climbed. Now looking down from the perch where I crouched to my landing pad, the daunting, dizzying space I was to fly through seemed much greater than I had originally anticipated.

After studying my options, and not wanting to humiliate myself before my younger brothers by backing out, I took a deep and tremulous breath and off I sailed into space. As calculated, I arrived at the edge of that worn stinky ole mattress, but I did not then leap off as planned in great triumph. No, I had landed with the toes of my left foot curled under and so I pitched forward with my face painfully slapping the muddy ground at the side of the house. Humiliated, I arose wiping my face with my otherwise useless cape and experiencing searing, excruciating pain in those four poor doubled up little toes. Never in my young life had I experienced such pain as I curled up writhing there on the ground. My frightened brothers ran for Mom, thinking I was dying, and truly I thought I might be. I didn't want to cry, despite the fiery pain, but tears suffused my eyes, blinding me, and moans escaped my clinched teeth. The King of the Jungle was downed.

When Mom showed up, she began berating us for such dangerous foolishness until she realized I might possibly be seriously hurt and needed to be gotten into the house and into bed. Now, Mom began to talk about calling the doctor, and I, despite the intense throbbing in my foot, realized things might now be getting totally out of hand. What I was remembering was that the family was planning on going on our first ever vacation together to Florida in a week or two, and I had better not mess up that opportunity by my stupid antics. I now begged; "Mom, please don't call the doctor. I will surely be O.K. in a day or two." When Dad got home that evening and saw my swollen and purple foot, he too was for calling the doctor. "Please, Dad," I begged, "it really looks worse than it actually is, and as you can see I didn't break my silly neck." And to prove it, I got up and limped about, leaning on everything I could and walking on the heel of my left foot. Though Dad laughed at this, he could not hide the concern on his handsome face. God, but that was painful; but by damn, I and the family were not going to miss that vacation to Pensacola on my account. Evidently Mom and Dad bought that I was not injured seriously, and so later, after a painful week of limping, we were all off on the train for exotic Florida and the warm salt waters of the Gulf of Mexico as planned.

In Florida we spent several days just soaking up the sun on that beautiful, white sandy beach and wading and swimming in that wonderful salt water. Glorious. Never before had we been to the sea, and it was a blissful experience for all of us. I began to just sit in the light surf and wiggle my toes; and so gradually walking began to be less painful, and I felt eventually my pain and difficulty would disappear.

When the Larkins returned from Florida, they plunged in earnest into preparations for their first experience of school in Amory, and they were anxious to get on with it. Jimmy, now six, would start in the first grade; Johnny, seven, would enter the second; Sammy, eight, would be in the fourth, all in the elementary school building; and finally Mary Ann, eleven, would start in the seventh grade, then being taught in Amory's high school building. The 1940–1941 school year would be the only year that Mary Ann would ever spend at school in Amory.

605 7th Avenue North, Amory, MS

Within days of school starting in the fall, our family made our second and last move in Amory, to a one-story, two-bedroom, one-bath wood frame house directly across 7th Street North and the town's elementary school. Here, located on the very northeast edge of town, our parents, with their lively young brood of three girls and three boys, were to live for the next exciting and challenging ten years.

Drennon "Dred" Davis, a long-time resident of Amory and recently retired railroad man known to Dad by his having worked for the Frisco, rented this house to Dad and Mom. Mr. Davis had heard that we were being ousted from our rental home because we were Catholics, and he took compassion on us. Note: Soon after we moved into this house we purchased it from Mr. Davis for $2,000 with $20 down and $20 monthly payments until it was paid off.

Going to School just across the street was a snap. We got up with Dad and shared with him a hot bowl of oatmeal with raisins and a glass of milk and off to our classes. Here I attended the fourth, fifth, and sixth grades and completed the seventh grade in the high school building two blocks to the south. At lunchtime we stepped across the street, where Mom had a sandwich and milk for us; then back to school till 3:30 or 4:00 pm. No miserably long cold, rainy, and snowy walks back and forth as in my first three years of school in Springfield, thank you!

My fourth-grade class was held downstairs in the school building, and about all I remember was the "spelling bees" which were held with us students standing against the wall. If we missed a word, we would have to sit down. I did rather well at spelling until one day our teacher told me that I should spell my words "just as they sound to you." From that day on, my spelling ability went out the window. For some reason this small mind of mine is exceedingly "literal," and I took instructions in that way, and with no modification—a true weakness.

As our play area during recess, the boys of our fourth-grade were assigned the north area of the school yard, just across from our house. Here for three years my brother Johnny and I were to endure almost continuous, unremitting harassment from our fellow male students. Kids can be cruel on a school yard and isolate, tease, and bully a child that is in some way different from the others. Well, these boys found many excuses to torment and persecute us. Brother Jim also joined us as an object of this torment a couple years later.

It all started with name calling, such as "Damn Yankee," this the most common and hated label, shouted at anyone coming into their southern community from the north, and thus one therefore responsible for their forefathers being humiliatingly beaten in the Civil War. "Carpet Baggers," was an insult flung at supposed opportunists coming from the North seeking to exploit and impose new rules on the South in the aftermath of the Civil War. "Nigger Lover" was their stinging remark castigating us for agreeing with President Lincoln's freeing of the Slaves and for our accepting Blacks as equals. And finally, "Catlickers," their damning Protestant reference to our being Roman Catholics who allegedly licked (kissed) the shoes of the Pope in submission.

This was the fetid social attitude we unwittingly found ourselves trapped in within this Southern, virtually one hundred percent Protestant white population, where, too, many we soon found, hated the above labeled groups to whom we proudly belonged. These labeled groups also included Jews, Blacks, Mexicans, Asians and other "foreigners," even though they might very well also be American citizens, as ourselves.

We were astounded and incredulous at the depth and virulence of their detestation of us. This storm came totally unexpectedly out of the blue. We had had no idea why this deep and prevalent prejudice and ignorance should continue to endure after so many years in this deep South, Confederate, Rebel town. We learned early why the Ku Klux Klan was so deeply rooted and alive and well in Amory.

How deep was this ignorance? One bizarre belief held that Catholic Priests, Nuns, and some Catholic laypeople, as emissaries of the Devil, had *cloven* feet. To this end, these boys once actually made me take off my shoes and socks to prove that I was a normal human being. These Johnny Reb boys made life at school miserable for us, torturing us in any and every way they could think of. Till then, we had never even heard of the Civil War; yet now we were forced to fight this historic tragedy practically every day we crossed the street. All this led to pushing, shoving and swinging of fists as well as sometimes two or more of the boys ganging up on one or another of us. I cannot recall during the three years that this went on that another boy ever stepped in to stop these attacks or, even more, that one of the teachers intervened or even any mention was made of what was going on. Evidently, the adults turned their backs and chose to be blind to what was going on in front of their very eyes. As I have said before, my Father was the most peaceful, loving, and gentle man I could imagine. Dad was also a brave, strong, and proud man. It had gotten to the point where he decided that we boys needed to learn to defend ourselves and when necessary to fight to protect ourselves and thus hopefully reduce some of this constant abuse.

Christmas of 1941 we boys received the gift of two pairs of regular boxing gloves; then followed by instructions on how to use them effectively. Dad had grown up the youngest of a Family of eight children. A brother, Uncle Jim, only two years older than Dad trained as a pugilist while a young man for the boxing ring, and our Father trained with him as his sparring partner. Our Dad had only occasionally climbed into the ring, yet he truly knew how to fight, and it was from him we received our lessons.

Woven through our training was a good deal of advice from Dad. "Listen, boys, never pick a fight with another kid especially if he is smaller than you. And if you are in a fight with someone not quite your size remember he may be more dangerous and surprise you by using other than fair means to compensate. You must use your skills only if you are provoked, attacked first, and have no way out from a corner." One suggestion he made was to stand me in good stead several times in the future: "When you are challenged by a group, let them know you would rather not fight, but if you must, then you will challenge the leader or the one who thought that he were the biggest, meanest, and toughest of the bunch and so thought they could beat you. This will help to level the field. Also select the leader if possible and attack swiftly, fiercely, and with everything you got, giving them no chance for an initial response. This tactic of surprise and fearlessness may often give advantage you might not otherwise have. If you can startle and stop them in this way, many times they will back off, not wanting to take a chance of losing face in front of their peers and be embarrassed by getting hurt or losing to you. It is a calculated gamble, but it is obvious you could never beat them as a group or even one after the other singly. You must awe them up front if you are to walk away with the least damage and with at least their begrudging respect."

The above became my plan, and with no help from authority and needing to protect myself and my two younger brothers, I needed drastic action. With these tactics, before long, the nasty tricks and bullying began to subside, and there was much less physical abuse. However we were summarily excluded from games and team sports and stood on the periphery of most communal activities, a pattern perpetuated almost totally during the time our family lived in this now detested Amory. The 1940–1944 school years were obviously not easy for us three little Larkin Boys, and we would never forget what we went through then and later in this Mississippi town.

An interesting story my older sister, Mary Ann, tells may help to point up how one-sided this kind of program actually was at that time. It seems that at the high school where she had her seventh-year classes (1940–41), there was a 'Prayer' broadcast over the P.A. system to all the classrooms every morning before class started. The young woman who selected the student to lead the prayer happened to be a friend of my Sister. This woman began importuning my sister to lead the prayer some time. Mary Ann astutely declined repeatedly, not only because she was a bit shy but also she had difficulty selecting a prayer she thought might be appropriate. Her friend was so insistent that finally my sister agreed to lead the prayer. The morning she stepped into the tiny booth and sat before the microphone to lead the little service; her mind momentarily went blank until, of a sudden, a prayer came to her and she began to recite "Hail Holy Queen, Mother of Mercy, our light, our sweetness, and our hope." At that moment in her recitation, the vice-principal leapt from his desk, heading for her booth, shouting furiously for her to stop. His loud interruption made her close and lock the door so she could complete the beautiful Catholic prayer to Mary the Mother of God she had begun. The red-faced vice-principal's shouting and pounding on the glass door went through the entire three story high school building and classrooms, causing quite an uproar.

When my young sister, only eleven years old at the time, finished her Prayer and opened the door, she was unceremoniously marched to the vice-principal's office with his shouting, "You are being expelled from this school, and never come back here again." This poor girl ran the two blocks to her home crying uncontrollably, hardly able to sob out what had happened to her to her now very upset Mother. Mary Larkin immediately called the school for an explanation, and when she learned the circumstances she then put in a call to the Educational Board in Jackson, the Capital of Mississippi. Within days Amory high School received a personal visit from a representative of the State Board of Education, instructing the school to reinstate this pupil, Mary Ann Larkin, and to make a public apology for their unprecedented, unjust, insulting, and uncalled-for discourteous treatment of this innocent student. Mary Ann finished that one and only school year (the seventh grade) there in Amory, but then left that town never go to school there again. The following school year my two brothers and I were also sent off to a Catholic boys Boarding School near Searcy Arkansas. For the rest of most of our school years, the only time we returned home was for Christmas and summer vacation. Forgive the French, but as far as we were concerned Amory, and all it hypocritically stood for, could go to hell!

Various Memories

Christmas Tree
Another extra we found for having our home on the edge of town was the delightful wooded area just a short hike from our place. Checking it out one fall day while catching fresh water crawdads hiding under rocks in a quiet little stream that meandered through the charming area, we came upon an area with a large number of various sized cedar trees. We found that some were just the right size and shape for our family's Christmas tree. I told nobody of my discovery, at the time, keep-

ing it a secret to be revealed as a surprise at the right moment. Was I a proud one as I swung my hatchet, cutting the perfect tree for our front room. I felt as a hero as I hauled this fragrant, deep green tree home for the holiday. My brothers and sisters and parents were delighted. And so each year thereafter it was left to me to search out the ideal tree. It was ever a surprise to me that the tree I had chosen months before was still waiting patiently for the moment of harvest—what a joy.

Pecan Harvest

One more way we three young boys harvested the bounty of the neighborhood came in the form of the pecan trees scattered about our town. These interesting trees can at full size produce bushels of rich sweet-meated nuts with relatively thin, hard skins, making it easy to enucleate the tasty fruit within. When we noticed these nuts beginning to fall, we knew gathering time had arrived. Here is how we operated. We knocked on the owner's door, asking, "Would you like for us to harvest your tree or trees?" Usually they would say, "Sure, but how much do you charge?" "Our deal is this: we'll climb into those tall, stiff branches as high as possible and shake every limb of their dried, hard-hulled incrusted nuts and then gather them up from the ground into equally filled sacks—one for you and one for us–as our pay." It worked almost every time, for it would cost them nothing out of pocket, and big folk would certainly not take their life in their hands up in those spindly, shaky, brittle branches. Now Mom would take the pecans we had hulled and shelled and make the most delicious pecan pie one could imagine. And you must know that the satisfaction we boys got from doing this job, bringing home this wealth of nuts, eating our fill and giving away of this abundance, was immense. We loved climbing those trees like three human squirrels.

Fishing

Mississippi summers also brought out our uncontrolled craving for fishing. Initially I think we used tiny white bread dough balls as bait, but mom frowned on this, so we began to dig for red worms to thread our hooks. Each day after our parents finished their coffee, we tossed the grounds out the back door into a small triangular flower bed area at the foot of our back steps. Those coffee grounds did more then fertilize the plants there, but helped, we soon discovered, to produce the biggest, fattest and juiciest, longest wiggling red worms you ever did see. And these found conveniently right there at our back door as we headed to the lake. Here we also tossed our dirty dish water, which kept that black soil moist and in just perfect condition for bait for those hungry perch, bream, and goggleye waiting for us down at our "private" lake. We learned early to clean those small, bony fish that Mom would then bread by dipping them into a batter she made of cornmeal or flour, a little milk and maybe an egg, and fry them to a crisp, golden brown for our dinner. Delicious, the fruit of our afternoon catch.

World War II

Sunday Dec. 7, 1941, "a day that will live in infamy," as President Franklin Delano Roosevelt declared to the

US Congress the next day, was the day the Japanese attacked Pearl Harbor. That quiet Sunday morning Dad, sitting in his favorite chair and I on my belly on the rug, were in the living room reading the newspaper and discussing local news while enjoying lovely classical music when suddenly a reporter broke into the program, shattering this peaceful moment with the astounding news that the Navy Port of Pearl Harbor in Hawaii had been bombed by the Japanese. It was like we were in a dream; it was just too unreal, and we were in shocked silence for a long few moments until I timidly broke it with the question, "Are we now going to war?" Dad's handsome young face was for the first time in my experience a pale gray and tired looking as he responded slowly, "Yes, Sammy, I don't think there can be any other way." I don't know where the rest of our family was at that time, but we, Dad and me, at that moment were frozen in inaction as we reflected on the enormity of the overwhelming news we had just heard with our hardly believing ears. Thus began that incredible time, the next long drawn-out four years, which our nations and the world refer to as WWII. For those of us who lived through this period, this war had a profound impact on our lives, in so many, many ways.

During WW II everyone with even the smallest parcel of land planted a "Victory Garden," not only for a patriotic reason but also for the wonderful experience of raising your own food and eating it, fresh, tasty, and vitamin filled. And for this produce you needed no food stamps or $$$, for that matter. Behind our house was a deep lot maybe 50 by 100 feet, and this became the Larkins' bountiful Victory Garden. A partial list of what we raised: potatoes (white and red), several kinds of leaf lettuce, cabbage, sweet potatoes, squash, melons, peas (green, black-eyed, and Crowder), string beans, butter beans, tomatoes, fresh corn, onions, beets, and other produce I can't even remember right now. I was given a patch to plant what became tall stalks with sticky itchy pods of okra which I sold for pennies to a local grocery store after Mom took what she wanted for the family.

This lot had been plowed harrowed and mounded by a black man following his ol' mule with ancient tools, a job he did for the entire neighborhood each spring. Then it was our turn to plant the different seeds in this rich, dark loam and cut chunks of potatoes, being certain there was at least one 'eye' on each piece before in was covered with the exact amount of soil. Now the big job in that garden was the endless boring hoeing, chopping, and weeding we all had to participate in. It was hard sweaty, work, but it was an education as well about soil, plants, seed, growth, food, and self-sufficiency which would stick with you for life. And then there was that glorious moment of harvest topped off by our enjoying our feasting together as a family around our dinner table each evening.

Mowing Lawns
In Mississippi it rained a lot, and in the rich, sandy soil we had, the grass and other plants grew abundantly, fast, thick and rank most of the year, giving us the opportunity of capitalizing on this situation. We had an old push mower Dad had cleaned up, oiled, and sharp-

ened. He also had an assortment of lawn tools we boys used to launch our "landscaping" business. We had an old straight blade "swing blade" with which we knocked down tall weeds and stragglers before we pushed and pushed till each lawn looked perfect to our "trained" eye. We trimmed hedges, edged sidewalks, cleaned out brush, working like little troopers for those few bucks that those good neighbors grudgingly parted with in their generosity. Initially our reward was a quarter here and there, but as we grew bigger and improved over the summers, our experience began to pay off with respect and referrals and more $$$.

One reason for our need for dollars was the family's tradition of yearly vacations to some, for us, exotic location or other. Here is a list of some of the places we visited on the train of a summer: Pensacola, Florida, and the Gulf coast; Kansas City and Springfield, Missouri; Houston, Galveston, and El Paso, Texas, as well as Juarez, Mexico and a side trip to Carlsbad Caverns, New Mexico; a trip to Colorado and Pike's Peak; a trip west across the continent to Los Angeles, Hollywood, and the Pacific Ocean. We children looked forward with the greatest anticipation to these exciting well-planed trips with our wonderful parents. Travel we found was always a wonderful experience and had for us a broadening effect.

Story Time
It seemed like every night it was a battle getting us three boys to bed. We loved sitting about the living room floor while Mom and Dad talked or Dad read and Mom knitted while we played board games, cards,

or worked on a puzzle or homework. Every evening, when it was time to go to bed, each one of us children would kiss Dad and Mom good night and slip under the covers. That didn't mean necessarily that we would then go right to sleep. Oh no! Johnny and Jimmy would now importune me, as their elder brother, to tell them a story. It didn't matter how tired or sleepy I might be, they would continue to insist till I would give in and begin with, "Once upon a time. . . ." Now I would begin a story that I made up as I went along, never knowing what was coming next. They liked scary stories and action stories and anything I could dream up. Sometimes they wanted me to continue a story I had been telling the night before, which I of course had not the slightest memory of. At times we got too loud, and then we would hear, "You boys quiet down in there and go to sleep." This could help to bring my story to an end, but not always. At times I could put them to sleep by gradually slowing my narrative down and lowering my voice. At other times I would get so tired myself I could hardly articulate and would begin to fall asleep. If Johnny was totally enthralled with my narrative, he would prod me to continue for more. This was almost a nightly ritual while we boys were young and still at home. Now I notice that my story is beginning to have its effect on y-o-u put-ti-ng y-o-u tooooo ssllleeep. . . . This nightly ritual we three boys missed when we entered boarding school in Arkansas in 1945. Yawn!

A Life-Threatening Incident at Work

It was a year of tragedy for our Family when our Father was scalded, almost to death, at work. I think it was about 1945, the year my two brothers and I were sent away to boarding school in Arkansas. Dad was working on the piping assembly found beneath one of those huge metal coal burning steam locomotives. The long narrow concrete pit work area underneath this engine was cold and clammy in winter and hot and grimy and stuffy in summer. Dad's job there, never comfortable at best and always heavy, dirty, demanding work, had always the element of danger added to this difficult and unglamorous job. Dad, working endlessly day after day with frequent over time demands and occasional emergencies, especially during the war years, never complained.

Safety was always paramount in this potentially dangerous work and was expected from all the many railroad employees. One day, while my father was engaged in working beneath one of these "live" engines, someone, unauthorized, slipped unnoticed into the cab of this locomotive and for some inconceivable reason pulled a lever that released a hellish roar of super-heated steam under incredible pressure onto my now trapped and broiling father, unexpectedly now fighting for his life. When this steam is released there is such an unbearably loud hissing sound, especially in an enclosed space, that it drowns out all other sound till it is finally shut off or is exhausted. No one could possibly hear my dear father's shrieks of agonizing pain over that blast, and only when the steam had been shut off did his fellow workers hear and discover the roasted moaning pile of barely alive flesh that was left of my father.

They dragged our Dad, hardly conscious, out of his *pit of hell* and immediately covered his back with "ginseng violet," which was then totally scraped off, with all the skin on his back, when they got him, barely breathing, to the hospital. He only survived because he happened to have had his back to that open steam pipe the instant that that fiery force of steam was released. Rushed to the town's primitive little hospital, the doctor had to cut off the now baked-on work shirt from Dad's back. Now they applied special ointment hopefully to soften, soothe and disinfect this completely raw, barely alive man's back. We were told later that the Dr. had said, "This man will probably not survive this terrible ordeal more than 24 hours."

It was a true miracle that our dad was to pull through this horrible ordeal. He was a strong, courageous man with a steel will and a purpose for survival. He was totally dedicated to his wife and six children, for whom he was their sole support. His will to live, his love and sense of responsibility, must have been the greatest forces to help bring him through this horrendous life-threatening crisis.

As soon as he began to improve, Dad insisted he be brought home—only a mile from the hospital—and there be lovingly be cared for by Mary, our mother. He had little confidence or respect for the staff and poorly equipped primitive Amory hospital. And in retrospect this may have been in part what helped to save his life. He needed round-the-clock loving care with constant changing of bandages and painful applications to prevent infection. How he endured the severe and ever-present pain and discomfort was marvelous. He could only lie on his stomach and could never quite find a position in which he could truly find rest. Sleep was always fitful, broken regularly for fresh bandaging or medication of various kinds.

As the endless weeks of his slow recovery dragged on, the blessed miracle of healing began to be taking place. Slowly, slowly Daddy began to resume those basic movements of his limbs and began again to sit up, to walk, and normally to relieve himself. God, the man was brave! His nobility shown in his patience and lack of complaint, his smile, and his ever expressed appreciation of the labor of those who worked for and with him in his recovery. Soon, with the help of Mother's constant exercising him as his therapist, he began to stretch and regain the use of his limbs and to walk, eat on his own, and resume more of the normal activities of a healthy man of 40. It seemed to take forever, at the time, but given his driving determination, the progress he made was phenomenal. Before long, actually much too soon, he began talking about going back to work— unrealistic as it was.

Our Father was one of those rarest of men, strong yet gentle, most accepting of others wheresoever they may have come from or their color or whatsoever might be their philosophy, politics, or religion. He was decidedly un-prejudiced and passed this on to his children. His obvious acceptance and respect for his fellow black co-workers must have been a constant burning reproof for his fellow white cohorts in these staunchly prejudiced—KKK—surroundings, and an ever-present indictment of their racial attitudes. Yes, the motivation may have been no more that to scare and warn our father, or it could have been more. The "accident" may have been pre-meditated, designed to eliminate our father and his family from this lily-pure Protestant, Confederate Southern Community, *for good.*

This heroic and dedicated man ultimately prevailed and again walked tall, with little or no outward evidence of the tremendous trauma he had endured and the personal burden he silently carried within due to his environment.

WW II Troop Trains

During the WW II years, 1941 to 1945, the railroads were obviously an active and essential component to the nation's success in the executing and winning of this overwhelming global conflict. Then it was constantly stressed that movement of troops and equipment of every kind must be ever a most top priority secret.

It must have been in 1942 or '43 when I was ten or eleven years old that Dad began to tell us boys when we might expect troop trains, trains exclusively set aside for the transfer of military personnel, coming through and stopping at our train station in Amory. We boys would jump on our bikes, dropping anything we were doing, as soon as we got our Dad's call, and race to the train station as fast as we could clear from the other end of town. Man, did we burn rubber! There we would greet these lonely young men with happy, smiling faces, cheering them up as best we could. Sometimes we had cookies that Mom had made to share with them. We

were young, enthusiastic and ready to perhaps be helpful for them in any small way we could to help lighten a
moment in their dull, boring, and lonely travel. Before
long they were requesting we run errands to the local
store for small items like cigarettes, gum, candy, and
other little things. A small hotel about 200 feet away
sold these type things, and here we raced with their
money so we could speed back and deliver before the
train moved off down the track. Most of the time we
got back OK, but occasionally the store would be busy,
and we would have to wait too long, then we might miss
the train leaving. Once or twice we raced back, having
to follow the slow moving train as it gained speed and
deliver the goods by tossing them from our moving
bikes through the windows to the soldiers in the moving cars. Exciting! Our failures were not many, but it
was a calculated risk, and we had to make split-second
decisions as to what to do. It was a bit nerve-wracking
but an exciting little service for the war effort, and we
felt we were helping in our small way. We had fun and
also picked up some pocket change as well. In all it was
a very exhilarating experience for my brothers and me
at that young and impressionable age.

It is passing strange, now on reflection, that we
never saw *even one* other kid offering their services or
even visiting the train to see the soldiers as they passed
through during those couple of years. The school years
of 1944–1945 and 1945–1946, my two brothers and I
went off for schooling to a Franciscan boarding school
in Arkansas, and so were home for the troop trains only
during the summers. I believe it was the last year of

the war that the ladies of the town finally organized their "canteen corps" to set up a hospitality booth with drinks and treats for the troops, and when we showed up back home that last summer, we were very firmly told we were unneeded. We were sad, but we realized we were now obviously superseded, not wanted, and redundant, and the job was now more than being taken care of by the lovely ladies. My sister recently sent me a picture cut from a copy of *The Amory Advisor,* dated 7–19–1944, showing a waiting troop train with soldiers on the steps and hanging out the windows and a couple of pretty local girls from the canteen corps passing out goodies. In one corner of the picture is a side shot of little Sammy Larkin, just watching, painfully aware he was now summarily dismissed, his moment of usefulness gone, so sad.

One of the most significant occurrences of this period was the birth of our third sister, Judith Catherine Larkin, on Nov. 16, 1943, in our own home. Mother chose to have her last child brought forth in her own bed surrounded by only her family, using as her midwife her dear friend, Mrs. Butler, a trained nurse. I shall never forget that marvelous, pungent effluvium that came forth and filled our entire house at the moment of birth that November afternoon. This last child, Judy, has ever brought great richness and joy to all she has come in contact with. Suffice it to say that we will treat her more fully as my little story proceeds. Welcome little Beauty into your loving family.

Anna Pinter

My families have always been great storytellers. As a child I listened with great interest to all the awesome tales about my ancestors. There was only one lady, a third cousin, who wrote some of the stories on paper. In 2001 I decided to take a writing class and record the tales I had heard as a young child. I started researching when I was ten years old, and had already verified many of these stories. The challenge is to record the tales for future generations because no one in my generation, my children or grandchildren, has taken more than a casual interest in family history. In the future there will be descendants who will be interested in the past, and my obsession is to record as many stories as possible.

Recently, I have begun to record more recent history because my grandchildren wanted to know about their grandparents and parents. They are reading these stories and have begun to read the ancient tales of our family settling in America.

I am a sixty-five-year-old a mother of three and grandmother of three. I graduated from college and taught school. I was forced into an early retirement and fought an illness for eleven years. As I began to heal, I returned to college and graduated with straight A's at the age of forty-four. After graduation I was unable, due to continuing health problems, to work as a fashion designer. I became a grand-mother and helped watch over my three grandchildren as they have grown into fine young children and adults.

My interest in genealogy has never waned for fifty-five years. I have written many stories about the lives of my ancestors. "Summer Evenings of My Childhood" is one of a series of stories about my life on my grandparent's farm in Illinois. It is my hope that my family will become interested in their history as they read about a time and place that is becoming extinct in America.

Summer Evenings of My Childhood

The summer evenings of my childhood, on my grand-parents' farm, were filled with wonderful sensory memories. The approaching dusk freed a new world of creatures and noises that were silent in the daylight. The grasshoppers, katydids, beetles and other small insects became silent, and the night air was filled with the reverberations of the locust and crickets. The hawks with the swooping sounds and distinctive voice disappeared, as did the crows with their crude caws. The predator of the night was the owl. The large barnyard owls and his smaller cousins tracked the scurrying rats and mice. Their whoo whoooo could be heard every night during the summer in the small grove of oak and sycamore trees behind the barn. There was another family of owls that lived in the forest beyond the cow pasture. If you listened carefully, the two families had a different voice. The only creature that was fairly safe and seldom eaten on those nights was the firefly. Their rear end gave off a light that would have made them a target for a tasty meal. However, they tasted terrible, and even a small beetle if it caught a firefly would start eating the head first, and discard the tail.

The firefly's main enemy on the summer nights in Indiana and Illinois were the children. My cousins Dennis, Harold, Katie, and I would carry big glass canning jars into the cow pasture. The pasture was the favorite playground of the fireflies. The boy firefly would flash the gal firefly, expecting to engage in a bit of fun. Suddenly his flirtation would be cut short, and both would find themselves trapped inside the jar looking out. Once they were inside the jar with several other fireflies, the light was so luminous we had a lamp to use for the evening. We would lie in the grass and talk about the cowboy movies. My hero was Hopalong Cassidy, the good guy, dressed in a black hat, and black cowboy outfit, white hair, and Topper his white horse. We would have long discussions about comic books, movies, swimming at the park, church, the constellations, what we wanted to be when we grew up, and other common things kids talked about. As we grew older we discussed the facts of life, and why one boy or girl was better to date than another. We compared our boyfriends and girlfriends and gave our opinions about what we thought were the important things in life. When we were in high school we discussed world affairs and the books we read, played games, and talked of how life would change as we went our separate ways. We should have been happy when our older cousin married, but we were sad. It was one more sign of the changing times.

The one pastime that did not change was catching fireflies. We were seventeen through thirteen, and we were still in the cow pasture chasing fireflies. We counted them to see who had the most, and then set our jars beside us and began to talk. This was the last carefree summer I spent doing kid things. I was in my sixties before three of the gang were together again in the same room. My cousin Harold I have not seen since he was fourteen.

The memories of Dennis as the protector, Harold as the ornery cousin, Katie as the shy one, and I as the outgoing organizer are still alive in my thoughts. How I wish I could get my cousins together on a sultry, humid Southern Illinois summer night and run through the cow pasture chasing fireflies. What fun it would be to lie on the cool grass and talk for hours with only the firefly lamps to light the night. This cannot happen. The homestead is gone, and the cow pasture has been planted in soybeans.

Going Home

When my mother and I went to visit relatives, in 1998, the first day was a happy gathering filled with eating, small talk, and reminiscing of old times. Although many of my relatives had not seen me in forty years, time had not changed our feelings for one another. Our conversations were as if we had seen each other yesterday. As we talked, all the barriers and excuses as to why I had not returned in such a long time seemed ridiculous and trivial.

While lying on my bed, the first night, my thoughts were "Who said you could never go home again?" The day and early evening had been exactly as the family gatherings of my childhood. While preparing to go to sleep, the memories of the hot nights sleeping in Grandma's feather bed came floating back into my mind. The bedroom was not air-conditioned, and the Southern Illinois night was the same as every summer night forty years ago. How many times had excuses been made for not returning? Sleep did not come easy as my brain mulled over all the experiences I had missed by being too responsible for my own family. Excuses crept into my mind, and in my dreams I began to relive the years and what was missed.

My eighty-eight-year-old uncle, no longer lived on his farm; he had moved to the small town on the west end of the five mile country road leading to my grandparents' farm. The large screened-in porch on my uncle's village home faced the beginning of the paved road. The morning would find me driving with great anticipation on the road to Snowdrop Hill, down into the valley, and going home to a time in the past. After a restless sleep, I was awakened by familiar smells coming from my aunt's kitchen. My aunt and mother were out of bed early and had prepared an old-fashioned farm breakfast of eggs, bacon, sausage, ham, biscuits, gravy, blackberry jelly, coffee, and fresh juice. It had been forty years since I had eaten a large breakfast, and it was impossible for me to be polite and eat the country feast. After the breakfast dishes were washed, my mother and I drove to Snowdrop Hill.

When I was a little girl, Snowdrop Hill was the most magical place in the whole world. My heart always skipped a beat when the car reached the top of the hill. Most of the countryside was flat, and the hill seemed so large. When the car reached the top of the hill there were only two smaller hills to pass by until we reached my grandparent's farm. The main roads were paved by the 1930s, but the roads between small towns were gravel. Many of the roads leading to the farmers' homes and fields were dirt. In the forties and the fifties the gravel road leading to my grandparents' home was only five miles long. My grandparents lived three miles from a small town with two hundred fifty population and two miles from a small town with less than two hundred residents. One town sat on the east end of the road and the other on the west end of the straight road. When you asked for directions, the residents always said, "Five miles as the crow flies."

Hour-by-hour, the hill changed as the angle of the sunlight shifted. No one else in my family could feel the magic. Every time I reached the top, the hill seemed to come alive. If the person driving the car were not in too big of a hurry, he would give in to my pleas and stop the car. The windows were rolled down so my senses could take in the magic. There were not many trees on the hills and in the valleys. The leaves of the small trees would pick up the wind, and the leaves made a whistling noise. On hot summer days, there was a quiet stillness on the hill. The trees were silent as was the rest of this magic kingdom. The animals began to appear in the early morning when the small drops of dew covered the flowers and grass. As the day grew hotter all the animal noises disappeared. A solitary crow flew over the countryside looking for food. You could hear an occasional small bird or insect scurrying on a humid hot day. As small cooling breezes crept in, during the darkness of night, the trees made little rustling sounds; animals hid and scurried about trying to avoid the night predators.

Most of the trees were long gone by the 1850s. The large trees had been cut to provide homes for the fast-growing population. A thriving wooden barrel business had supplied coopers with work for many years. As the trees dwindled many families moved to Missouri, where the cypress trees were plentiful, and the coopers could make their barrels.

When the car engine would start, my imagination would go back to the family tales of long ago in Illinois. The tales were of a virgin forest filled with dangers and adventures. The hills and valleys were a mystical kingdom where deer, bears, and mountain lions were plentiful, and Indians roamed the wilderness. My imagination would run wild as we drove down the county road, and I could see the renegade Indians ready to slaughter us before we reached home. I remembered the story of the ten-year-old pioneer girl who saw Indians and ran full steam for one mile. She almost died from fright. Her father and the other settlers caught the Indians and killed them. The same little girl heard a woman crying, and when she went to investigate came face to face with a mountain lion. She became frozen to the spot where she stood. The mountain lion was scared stiff, and in a short while walked away. All the old stories were real and grew bigger in my mind. No one seemed to understand my fascination with the hill. Grandma said, "You are an old soul, and you see many things other people do not see." Grandma was the same as everyone else; when the car stopped on the hill, she saw no magic.

Even if the hill had not been magical, there was beauty in the landscape. Every day the colors changed. On a clear spring day, the sky was bluer and the grass greener. The color of the sky hinted an approaching spring shower or a balmy windy day. The colors were never just one hue. The grass and trees were always multicolored. Dried weeds and flowers left over from many seasons ago were woven into the new green spring growth. There were no mowers to manicure the countryside. An occasional cow or other farm animal chewed away the growth, but nature and time were usually responsible for the landscape changing. The hillside in the summertime became dryer, and the colors were yellowed greens, wheat, and shades of rust. The skies were beautiful with large white billowy clouds that stretched to heaven. Grandpa would pray to the clouds. He would say, "See the clouds and pray for rain." Whenever a big cloud appeared over the hills and valleys I always prayed for rain. Whenever the rain fell the valleys and the hills turned greener and everything grew taller, Grandpa would say, "See you are taller. The rain made you grow a whole inch." The farmers who farmed the land were happier. As a young child I did not realize how important rain was to a farmer and attributed the magic to the rain and the hill. As fall approached, the landscape changed to a darker brown. The beautiful flowers and colorful grass disappeared, but the mystical creature that painted the leaves with bright hues of red and yellow replaced the colors. The fall colors lasted until the first rain, and then the bright, colorful leaves were knocked to the ground so nature and time could return them to the soil. In winter the snow fell covering all of Southern Illinois. Sometimes big dark clouds would come from the north and the wind would blow in snow. Life changed on the farm the minute the first snow fell. There were the tasks of feeding the animals, milking the cows, and other everyday tasks, but life became slower. Grandpa did not have to farm the fields and gather the crops. He would sit by the coal heating stove. Grandma made quilts during the winter. She loved to tell the story about my eating the loose threads that fell on the floor while she was quilting. Grandma always laughed as she told how many different threads were found in my diaper. Her quilts were very colorful and seemed to replace the colors of the white countryside. The snow brought the families together. Travel was impossible when the snowfall was deep. Family members would walk or drive over in a horse drawn sleigh. The men would whittle a stick and discuss *The Farmer's Almanac*. The ladies were seated around a quilting frame, sewing the tiny stitches, eight to an inch, which held the layers of the quilt together. This was a time for the ladies to relax before the life on the farm became more hectic in the springtime.

Sunday was different. *Come hell or high water,* the family went to church. A trip to church was not an easy task in the winter. The church was eight miles from the farmhouse. We were bundled into a car or a sleigh and traveled over the treacherous roads. The worst roads were where a layer of rain was frozen overnight, and dry snow fell early in the morning turning the earth into a large skating pond. The family never missed church.

New snow always gave me a mystical feeling when I was standing atop Snowdrop Hill. The breezes were crisper, and the cold air was cutting. The sounds echoed off the trees as their icy branches played music on the wind. The crisp dry snow crackled under my feet. The winter sounds replaced the insect and frog summer orchestra. When I told Grandma there was music in the winter snow and wind, she smiled and said, "Your old soul is hearing music from winter fairies and elves."

As most adults grow older, many of the magic and mystical feelings disappear. Grandma always said I was an old soul. Fairies and mystical creatures still exist for me because I refuse to surrender my beliefs.

Why did I return to Illinois after a long absence? In 1998 my mother insisted we take a trip and see the relatives. She informed me she was getting older, and she wanted to make sure she saw her brothers before they died. Mother had never laid a guilt trip on me, and she probably did not realize what she had done. She had given me an ultimatum, and there was only one answer. We arrived in August and drove to Evansville to visit my seventy-eight-year-old uncle. We stayed a few days and then started our sixty-five mile journey to my mother's birthplace. The August weather was no surprise, and was exactly like my childhood memories: hot, humid, and smothering. The first day was filled with small talk and reminiscing old times with my uncle and mother's eighty-eight-year-old brother's family. The next morning we began the short three-mile trip to my grandparents' farm. When we reached Snowdrop Hill, my heart skipped a beat, and magic filled the air. There were the small hills and valleys of my childhood. The hill was smaller than I remembered, but the magic still existed. When I exited the car, the warm, humid air wrapped me in a potpourri of scents and sensations. A crow glided over the smaller hill below. The leaves and the entire world had a mid-day silence. "Mama, do you feel the magic?" I asked. She looked at me and said, "Magic, what magic?"

Reluctantly, I left Snowdrop Hill and drove down into the valley. The drive to my grandparents' farm was a long mile. When we arrived at the farm, the farmhouse did not exist. The house was gone, as well as, the barn, chicken coops, garage, pigpens, garden, and all signs of human life. There were no animals, creek, fences, or wells, and the woods were missing. Many times my ears had heard, the beautiful old-fashioned farmhouse was gone, but my brain did not compute this fact until my eyes stared at the field of corn standing on my grandparents' front yard. There was corn in the field as far as the eye could see. A sense of great loss washed over me, and I knew, you couldn't go home again. Forty years were too long to carry memories in my heart, and all the excuses in the world would not erase the feelings of loss.

After Grandma went to her resting place no one lived in the family home. The estate was divided among her three living children. The homestead sat empty, and the spring rain, summer heat, fall frost, the winter freeze and snow faded the bright white paint. As the weathered planks were exposed to the elements, the porch began to sag. The warm family kitchen and living room became cold empty caverns. The screened porches closets, and pantry were hollow, echoing caves. Skunks, snakes, and other small creatures took refuge under the porch and foundation.

The area succumbed to the drug culture of the seventies, and druggies took refuge in the decaying rooms. Faded wallpaper peeled off the walls, and mice made their homes in the debris. City dwellers came with large trucks, in the dark of night, and stole the brass cabinet fixtures, decorative ceiling lights, and the brass, old-fashioned front door knocker. The thieves ripped up the solid oak floors. The beautiful stained glass windows and doors were removed, leaving gaping holes for the rain, snow, and the termites to eat away at the grand old house.

Still the house stood and refused to fall down. Finally in 1995, my uncle burned the house. He felt the dilapidated structure was a safety hazard and a magnet for trespassers. The house had stood empty for twenty-three years refusing to surrender to neglect and abuse.

Other houses on the surrounding farms have met with the same fate. The young people have left the farmlands, and reside in the surrounding cities. The new generations are not farmers, and their families do not live in the grand old homes, so the structures fall into disrepair and are destroyed.

While traveling the country roads in Southern Illinois, I looked into the fields and saw the old, decaying farmhouses. The houses refused to fall down and appeared to have taken on the spirit of their past residents. They are as strong and hardy as the pioneer men and women who struggled and survived in an impossible land of swamp and wilderness. These pioneers tamed the wild frontier and lived to see their world change. Grandpa would have been sad, because only one of his twenty-two grandchildren farms the land. However, Grandma would say, "It is as it should be. Life moves on."

The First House My Dad Built

I was raised on a small, five-acre piece of land in Indiana. My father was not much of a farmer and except for being a superb upholster and guitar player, he used very few of his talents. Our house was little more than a shack built of concrete blocks and fiberboard on the inside walls. There were two rooms downstairs and an upstairs loft. As a child I often wondered why anyone would build a house of gray concrete blocks. Not only were the blocks ugly but also when it rained and snowed the water seeped into the concrete and dampness permeated the whole house. It was a bone-chilling dampness that could not be overcome by the black potbelly stove that stood in the middle of the room that served as a kitchen and a living area. The floor had no covering, and gravel was the only material separating our family from the bare earth. The house was not fit for human inhabitance, and the only creatures who enjoyed our family dwelling were the mice, rats, spiders, and snakes. When the cold damp weather started in the fall, these creatures came into our house. I guess life was better inside for them than in the damp, cold outdoors of an Indiana fall and winter. They stayed until spring was over, and when gentler rains stopped, most of the creatures left our home. The outdoors was more inviting in the summer than inside our house. In the summer, the weather was humid, and the windows were not covered with glass or screens. When the rains stopped the window coverings came down and opened our house to mosquitoes, flies, and all creatures of the insect world. The coverings for the windows in the winter were brown paper soaked with bacon fat. You could not see outside but the snow and rain did not come inside. When the bacon fat began to wear off, my dad would put up a new sheet of brown paper. Once when I complained about the lack of glass windows, Dad said, "Just be glad we are not as poor as those who have to eat their bacon fat and have none to put on paper for their windows." Many times I thought about those people who were poorer than my family. I could not imagine how anyone could be worse off than I was during those bleak winter days.

The outdoor creatures liked to inhabit our house. The way the structure was constructed made a perfect hiding place for the varmints. The concrete blocks were covered with a fiberboard, and between the two layers all kinds of creatures dwelled. There were the mice who chewed the inside layer of the fiberboard and made little nests for their babies. I was only five when I spent my first winter in this house my father built. At night the mice chewed on the fiberboard walls and scurried across the loft floor. This did not seem normal to me as I had spent time in my grandmother's house, and there were no mice. She had three cats that killed the mice. Grandma would have never allowed the filthy critters in her home.

My oldest brother always had an ornery streak from the day he was born. He was only two and a half and enjoyed tormenting the little gray babies that lived in the storage place and in the walls. One night I heard screaming, and the adult mice had attacked my brother's ears. The rest of the winter he slept in the same area as my mother and father. The mice never showed aggression toward me. I always believed they attacked him because he was so mean to their babies.

The mice were the best creature that came to visit during the winter and the spring. The spiders were as big as the mice. Some were brown with round hairy bodies and built elaborate webs. There were black ones with hard, shiny long legs and colorful bodies. The spiders would fight for their space and many times they would eat one another. Sometimes I felt like the spider, wanting to fight for a small space away from the younger children and the house I hated.

The spiders stayed in the walls because they had everything they needed to exist. They had a nice space between the concrete blocks and the fiberboard. There were plenty of juicy bugs to eat and more warmth than was offered outside. While many times I went hungry, the spiders lived rather well. Once I watched in amazement as a spider chased a small mouse across the room. I still wonder if the spiders in our house ate mice. I thought even the spider had a better life than myself.

The gravel floor on the first story of the house provided little protection against the rain and melting snow. The dampness came through the dirt and made the rough stones cold. There were no rugs to cover the small stones, and I could feel the rough texture through my ugly black shoes. Snakes came in and wrapped themselves around the table legs of the kitchen table. They were harmless garter snakes and only came during the cool nights of spring. In the summer, due to the lack of glass windows, the mosquitoes buzzed in my ears. In the morning small itchy red patches covered the parts of my body that became uncovered during the night. I was never as afflicted by mosquitoes as my brother and Dad. The mosquitoes liked to suck their blood, and I thought my Dad deserved the bites because he built the "stupid" house.

There was no indoors plumbing, but my Dad purchased a toilet. He put it on a wooden platform about six inches high. The base of the platform was about three feet by four feet in size. The toilet sat there, and no walls were ever built around the base. There was never any plumbing attached to the toilet. Many times

I would sit and stare at the fixture setting in the corner of the downstairs bedroom. I would repeat over and over, "When I grow up, I am not going to be like him." I did not understand how someone could live with so little pride. I marveled at his talents. He could play the guitar and sang "Whispering Hope," "Amazing Grace," "Red River Valley," and "You Are My Sunshine." He could draw pictures and knew the answers to every history lesson. He was a craftsman who could upholster a King Louis davenport and restore the period piece to its original state, but we had no furniture in our house. There was a wooden kitchen table and six chairs. The table was not ordinary; it was a beautiful oak period piece with claw legs that resembled lions. The six chairs were matching and had the same lion clawed legs and red velvet cushions on the seats. Dad went to antique stores, and occasionally a piece of furniture came into our house. There were no living room chairs or sofas, and wooden fruit crates served as furniture. He made beautiful furniture but sold every piece to the rich folks in town. He never charged what his handicraft was worth, and so during World War II he was forced to work in a factory in order to put food on the table for his growing family.

My bed was an antique poster bed. It never had a lace canopy but was very beautiful. The four posters were large, carved wooden pineapples. The bed had a comfortable mattress and Grandma had given me two warm quilts. In the winter my bed was the only haven of warmth and comfort in the hated house. When I was eight years old my mother went to Southern Illinois to visit my grandmother. She was pregnant and said she needed her mother's help as she was always tired. My father took great exception to my mother's leaving and made his feelings known. He yelled and screamed, but my mother left and did not return until spring. When I walked into the house, my ornate old oak bed had vanished and only the mattress lay on the stark wooden loft floor. The house was empty, and there was not one piece of furniture. The table and chairs were gone, most of the summer clothes were missing, and not even the wooden crates were in the house. In his anger, Dad had burned everything we owned. We did not own much, but it was all gone. The only thing we now owned was the ceramic toilet. It still sat in the corner of the first floor of the hated house on its pedestal. All I could think was that summer was coming and maybe I would visit my grandparents' house before another winter. This was the last summer I spent in Indiana. When I was nine years old my mother sent me to live on my grandparents' farm every summer until I went to college.

Life in Indiana was very different from my grandparents' comfortable farmhouse, and I dreamed all winter of climbing into my uncle's fast moving car and leaving behind my Indiana life to spend the summer in Southern Illinois. I was born on the downside of advantage, the oldest of five children. My parents did not have the money to support one child and themselves, but as my mother said, "My children are all I have in life." This was true, but I never understood why she lived with my father.

Forgiving Father

When I was twenty-two I forgave my father for being himself. I decided my father was not a bad man. After much soul searching, I decided life had not prepared him to take care of himself, and he certainly was not prepared to be a father. When he chose my mother as a wife, it did not improve her situation. He was twenty-nine and she was twenty years old. Mom had lived on a very successful farm all her life. She had never lived in a city. My mother always said, "He didn't even know what a hollyhock was." Dad said, "She did not know how to turn on an electric light." They had no common ground of communication. He married her because she was beautiful, and she never figured out why she married him. His brother was married to her cousin, but Mom said this did not influence her choice. Mom would have learned quickly how to be a city girl, but my Dad was not a good mentor.

My father was still living with his parents in Anderson, Indiana. He was twenty-nine years old. The only reason I can figure out why he was living in his parents' home was because Dad was damaged. His mother and father lived a very strange life. They had raised five boys, and the stories from their West Virginia roots to Anderson, Indiana could fill a book with strange unbelievable tales. It was not that they were terrible people, but their psyches were scarred.

Mom has said once or twice maybe she was looking for something different. She always said, "I sure got something different, your father and his crazy rela-

245

tives." The animals on my mom's Illinois farm lived better than she lived during the forty-nine years of her marriage to my father. When I asked her after he died if she loved him, she said, "It was hard to with all the crazy, silly things he did." She never said for sure if she loved him or not. I figured it must have been love or this would make my mother even stranger than my dad.

There is always an argument: is it nature or nurture that makes a person who they are? Is it their gene pool or their environment? My father's gene pool was in relatively good shape. He lived to be only seventy-eight. He died, of all places, in a Jacuzzi. He had lived most of his life in one shack or another until the last part of his life. My parents had sold off all the properties my mom had bought with her inheritance and moved into a resort complex. The townhouse was in an upper-class neighborhood with golf courses, swimming pools, tennis courts, and four-star hotels. Dad did not play golf, swim, or play tennis, but he seemed to enjoy the Arizona lifestyle. It never snowed and the sun shone almost all the time in Phoenix. So one more crazy twist in my father's life. A man who lived in poverty most of his life makes a decision to enjoy a Jacuzzi by himself and drowns.

Dad was a brilliant man. He seldom showed his God-given intelligence. I learned one fact early in life. A person can be very smart and lose the ability to have common sense. I understood how smart he was and gave him credit, but no one else realized he was intelligent. They would always say, "It is a good thing Russell is good with his hands."

When I was older, I had a bit of fun with my brothers and sisters. In the 1980s one of my children bought the game Trivia. My son was superior at remembering every detail, big and small. He made a great partner when playing the game. My choice for a partner the first time all the family played together was my father. We had a great time playing. Our score was so much higher than everyone else's. Dad said, "We skunked them." They said we cheated. Dad said, "Play again." He knew every history question, every literature answer, could reply to all political trivia, and only on the sports questions did he falter. He knew his baseball, and we were lucky with the cards we drew. Dad only had an eighth grade education and had said many times he had been in six schools by the time he started third grade.

My father was always honest. When I was angry with him, my grandmother would remind me that at least I had an honest man for a father, with an unblemished name. He could cuss a blue streak. He cussed the world, God, his situation, the weather, a bad cup of coffee, his factory job, and almost everything in his life. He was an angry man damaged from his past. He was unable to find the skills to move on with his life.

His personality blew from calm to red-hot temper in a second. He was by nature a sensitive creative person. His artistic endeavors were amazing. He could pick up a watercolor brush and paint wonderful pictures. Most people have to practice watercolor every day, but not my father. He would paint, and the pictures were perfect. When he was finished he would tear them up. Dad played a 1928 Martin guitar and could sing beautiful songs and church hymns. When I was eight years old, he put the guitar away and never played again. He did not know how to give to his family, but could give to a perfect stranger or someone richer than he his last dime.

He never hit my mother. He sure had batting practice with his children. Some of his children were smarter than others. If you cried, he stopped. I never had the sense God gave a flea. I took it as a challenge until I was sixteen years old. I let him know that if he touched me again, it was a fight to the death. I guess he believed me and found someone else to release his anger upon.

Living with him was like a battlefield. When I was a child, I could not hate him, but I could not love him. No one in our house blamed my mother. She probably deserved some of the blame for not protecting us. She should have left him, but she did not. She lived in the shacks, found food even if she had to buy three eggs instead of a dozen. She raised a garden, canned, and endured the hardships with little complaint.

When I was sixteen years old, things began to change if only a small fraction. We moved into town. The house was not a fancy place. It was brand new and had a furnace and indoor plumbing. Mom put in nice beige carpeting. My Dad walked into the house with his muddy work shoes. When mom asked him to remove his shoes, he immediately threw a temper tantrum. He started wrecking the house. The carpet was torn beyond repair. I guess this was a breaking point for my mother. She used the money she had saved to buy the house, and now it was a mess, nothing more than a shack. What happened was this incident had unleashed my mother's tongue. She tongue-lashed him, and from that day forward made it clear she was taking none of his crap. He had been working a job at the factory. She took every paycheck. She nagged him when necessary and when it was not necessary. Very little changed! The tension was higher and sometimes the fallout of that tension was disastrous. There was very little peace and quite. I rather enjoyed the situation, and was glad to see him get his just deserts occasionally. My mother had been so quite all those years, and it was a real surprise to see how proficient she was at being a nagger. I guess he had stepped over some unknown mark in the sand.

I went away to college. He told me, "Our family can try to reach the top, but none of us will ever succeed." He had just given me one of his many challenges. The bullheadedness that my grandmother talked about kicked into full gear. I was totally unprepared to enter an academic world but I knew I had to succeed. My father did not want me to go away to school. He insisted I stay at home and commute. I let it be known I would walk the twenty miles to school if necessary. My father relented and drove me to college. He helped me find a room and a job. My mother gave me ten dollars every week. My rented room cost six dollars. Whenever I came home, she scraped together a bit of food for me to take back to school.

It was after I was married before I forgave my father. One day while reading a book it occurred to me that my anger was destroying me in much the same way my father's anger had destroyed him. My father had stopped fighting to win. He always expected to fail. If he was winning in a card game, he lost on purpose. I decided in a split second that he was winning, because of my anger toward him. Since that day I harbored no anger toward him. I only have one regret: that I did not realize who he was sooner. I am not making excuses for him because he is my dad. It just took me a long time to realize that life can beat some people up so they never recover from the beating. I would not have wanted to live with Dad's mother and father, but I guess my bullheadedness would have made me a survivor. Is it nature or nurture that makes us who we are? I do not know. It is one of those questions I have never been able to figure out. The one thing I do know: being bullheaded is an asset.

Art Weiland

I started writing in October, 2002, in the Writing Workshop at age 81. I did this because my wife died in March, our two children long ago fled, married, had children, and divorced, and although always busy, I was looking for an outlet. Up until then I had written only a few letters and engineering reports when in college. I do not read books, maybe seven during my lifetime. I graduated as a Mechanical Engineer and worked for Douglas Aircraft/ McDonnell Douglas designing hardware for military and passenger aircraft, anti aircraft missiles, space vehicles, and manned spacecraft for forty five years.

Since starting in the writing workshop I have written 74 pieces about my family and me that hopefully can someday be assembled into an autobiography for my family and future generations. My initial intent was that the workshop leader would teach me a little about writing. Actually, I was overwhelmed by feedback on my writing from all members of the workshop, plus the leader. This feedback improved my writings, provided incentive to continue writing, and taught me how to critique writings.

I make each writing a short factual story that my fellow writing workshop members might find interesting.

Hats

Stell had a thing about hats that was endearing to all her friends, but I never paid much attention until I looked back and could see how much it was a part of her.

Figure 1. Her winter hat in Chicago in 1930.*

Initially she was a conventional hat wearer. I wasn't there at the time; however, a picture of her winter hat in 1930 and a communion headdress in 1932 were a good beginning of this hat chronicle. There can be no doubt, that at her age, her mother made the selections; nevertheless, I could imagine a traditional hat revolt brewing in Stell, leading to later developments. When we started going out together, it was winter, windy Chicago; consequently, her headgear reflected those conditions.

Figure 2. Dressed for communion two years later.

Figure 3. A fur coat and hat to match in
winter of 1946.

I would be remiss to not include the wedding since
she was breathtaking in her veil. I can almost see her
walking down the church aisle, escorted by her father,
her face misty looking through the veil; then after the
wedding vows we sealed them with a kiss (after she lifted the veil to let it float down her back).

Figure 4. The following year a wedding in Chicago.

Figure 5. Mrs. Arthur Weiland in a car
leaving the church. In 1947.

She called a scarf tied over her head a babushka—
that I had never heard of, so I assumed it was Lithuanian terminology. It was the normal head piece for the
women in her Lithuanian Catholic church, though I
believe she always wore a hat. In Figure 7, she is trans-
planting sweet peas at Camp Adair. Even at Camp
Adair on Sunday she brought out a hat.

Figure 6. Stell gardening wearing a babushka in Oregon at our first home on a cool day.

Figure 7. One of her Sunday hats at Camp Adair,
even with no church.

The coming event was my graduation, and she had
the hat for the occasion. It turned out to be a hot day
with all the pomp and ceremony outdoors; as a conse-
quence, a brimmed hat would have been better, but I
believe she wanted something closer to my graduation
cap.

Figure 8. She made this special hat for my graduation.

Figure 9. Our move to sunny California inspired her making of this wide-brimmed sun hat.

After we bought our new house and got settled in, Stell started her hat making project. I don't know if she went to a hat class, but I suspect hat making was in her genes. She was prepared. On a couple of our visits in Oregon she had easily talked my Dad out of pheasant, duck, and geese feathers, plus fly fishing lures, called flies. Dad, of course, showed us around the local country, which was her opportunity to collect

Figure 10. This is one of my favorite hats because she looked pretty in a black hat with handcrafted yellow flowers made for Sunday church.

dried wild flowers and weeds. "You make hats out of all that stuff?" You bet and more, I don't know what, from the craft stores. At least she didn't use vegetables or fruit. Figure 10 and all the rest of the following are pictures of hats she made. Of course, I never took a photo of many other hats. Actually, I wasn't taking pictures of her hats, but of her. These photos are cropped to show mainly hats. One photo I wish I had was of an

Figure 11. This was Stell's favorite pink
party hat.

all multi-colored pheasant feathers hat. I won't attempt
to describe her hats other than by the pictures. Where
did she store them? That small house had four closets
that eventually were bulging with hatboxes.

Stell wore one of her hats every Sunday to church.
She came to be known as "Hat Lady of Moore Street."
She was a knockout in church, at least I thought so.

When we moved into our second home, she ceased
making hats; fewer and fewer women were wearing
them in church or otherwise, as we proceeded into the
following generation. I still have three of her hats that

Figure 12. She made this orange creation for our son's wedding.

I retained rather than giving them away. They are not in hat boxes; they are in the family room as part of the decor. The left over feathers and what not, all gone.

NOTE

* The photographer for Figures 1 and 2 is unknown. All the rest of the photographs are by Arthur Weiland.

My Dad

I was proud of my dad and always thought he was the best around, even though he was very strict, I'm sure a result of his war experience and being an army officer. I suppose that was good for me, but I never had such a notion when I was growing up.

Here's a small look into Dad's character. I was always fascinated by how he attacked a grapefruit. He had a sharpening stone used on a certain knife that sliced through the center of a grapefruit like him slicing a caught fish. With a stainless steel serrated, slightly curved knife he cut around the inside perimeter of the grapefruit and then meticulously slit each side of the dividers to separate the segments. After eating the segments, my interest peaked when he assaulted the pulp adhering to the skin. With concentration and a strong grip on the spoon, he went around and around and around, scrapping off and scooping up the remaining grapefruit juice until every drop was gone.

Going fishing or hunting for my dad was not a simple operation. The day before, he planned it like a military operation and had the car all loaded the night before. I think he was addicted and lived for the next outing. He never missed an opportunity to include fishing when we vacationed in Wisconsin or lived in

Washington and Oregon. Even when we moved from Illinois to Washington by car, he figured out a way to stop in Yellowstone National Park to fish in a stream.

I think he hoped he could make me a fisherman, but he didn't; however, I enjoyed going with him and witnessing his enthusiasm. He was a first-rate teacher, instructing me how to fly fish, to troll, or to sit still in a boat. He also taught me to row and to run the outboard motor to the best fishing advantage.

While we lived at Fort Lewis, Washington, this was a typical one-day fishing trip in 1936. We got up about 4:00 a.m., him eager and bushy-tailed, me dragging. We grabbed a quick breakfast, our sack lunches, prepared the night before, and took-off for Tacoma to one of the piers jutting out towards Puget Sound. On the way we didn't talk, but he pulled the squirrel up my pants leg trick with, "Gotcha," a grab on my thigh, and a laugh under his breath. The sun was just below the horizon, and the few lights were glowing through a very light mist. He cautioned me about the wet planking. He purchased a bucket of bait and we made two trips with all the gear, including his old two-cylinder, two-cycle outboard motor with enough power to barely get above trolling speed. He was meticulous in keeping it in running order and cleaning off the oil. A small rowboat was in the water with its bowline tied that Dad had reserved a day before. He carefully boarded with the motor and clamped it on the transom. He appointed me chief engineer since I didn't have a fishing license. With the gear loaded, bow line free, I filled the tank, primed the outboard, wrapped a rope around the flywheel, pulled like crazy, and adjusted the throttle. After two or three pulls it might start. He was a good teacher; eventually it started. The entire boat vibrated, blue smoke trailed out behind in the still moist air, and I could barely hear Dad's commands above the noisy outboard motor with no muffler.

"Slow down here," he yells after he readied his fishing pole with live bait skewered on a large hook. His hands were weathered, with heavy looking fingers that were uncommonly deftly handling the bait. I recalled how those clumsy looking fingers easily made fishing flies from feathers, thread, and what-not. His old crumpled hat had a couple of flies stuck in, and the floppy brim concealed his large bushy eyebrows, but not his alert brown eyes and large flattened nose from his university days as a football player. He let the line out over the side, and I could see the flashing of the chrome plated spinner then disappearing aft of the transom. He was silent, except telling me where to steer, and deep in concentration. There were a few other fishing boats in the area, and Dad seemed to know where to troll.

Free Flight I

This is not about obtaining free flights on commercial aircraft. In this era of radio controlled cars, boats, airplanes, and balloons, many youths don't know what "free flight" is.

When my dad was stationed at Fort Lewis during my junior year in high school (1937), I occasionally walked two miles out to the military airfield to look at the few Douglas observation high-wing aircraft. I was addicted to aircraft in any form. I didn't know a single soul who had the slightest interest in aviation, so I soaked up every page of the monthly model airplane magazines *Flying Aces* and *Model Airplane News;* I had scraped up enough nickels to order by mail. The articles about stability in flight and how to adjust the flight surfaces drew my attention. Five years ago my failed attempts with flying models were overshadowed by all these successful modeling guys in the magazine. I had to try again with an advertised gas powered model kit, an ambitious, costly project. I was impressed by the six-foot, tapered fore/aft adjustable wing, the cowled, inverted engine placement, the open cockpit, and the classy shaped tail surfaces. Somehow I managed to get my dad to pay for the gas powered engine, which I selected from the magazine ads and ordered by mail, along with bankrupting my savings to order the model kit I singled out.

"Free flight." If you ever folded eight-and-a-half by eleven paper into a glider and launched it from your hand, that was "free flight." The balsa wood, paper-covered model was more sophisticated, but entailed the same challenges of stability and adjustment, just more dollars and time if it crashed. The kit was a bunch of balsa strips/sheet, piano wire for base notes bent to form a flexible support for the wheels, paper for covering, and the plans. No dope, cement, or wheels. After barely starting construction, we moved to Medford, Oregon. That opened my modeling world with an airplane model store, a model club, and two guys thinking about building a gas powered model. It took about one year for me to build the model. In the meantime my model airplane buddies Buck and Dallair got started, finished, and were flying at the Medford airport after convincing the manager to allow launching off a taxi-way which connected the two parallel runways. In those days the airport was weeds beyond the asphalt paving, a small wooden hangar with two airplanes inside, and maybe during the day one airplane would land or take off.

I bought in-flight batteries and battery box to power the ignition system, a coil to provide high voltage for the spark plug, a condenser, an air timer, wheels and fuel. The timer was a cylinder and spring powered piston with an adjustable air bleed, and a piston activated switch to time the engine run. The fuel was a mixture of clear untreated gasoline available at the gas station and caster oil. Black tissue paper was bought, cut into big block letters, and doped to the wing for my name, "Thunderbird." I think our neighbors heard the thunder part. When starting the engine, a large three-volt "booster" battery with wiring was clipped to the sparkplug, since starting the engine could require one to twenty minutes of priming the cylinder and flipping the prop with your finger. But watch that prop; many fingers have been cut by spinning props. After several days of trying and then getting the engine to start and run reliably, then establishing the moveable wing position in relation to the center of gravity, my mother drove me to the airport with the back seat full of airplane.

Free Flight I

I fastened the wing with rubber bands; the tail surfaces, with a small rudder tab, were cemented on during construction, so no dethermalizer. (More about
that later; it hadn't been invented yet). I joined Buck
and Dallair on the taxi strip. Now was time for the
anxious, gut-wrenching first flight. . . Would it stall on
take off and crash on its nose or claw its way into the
sky, then when the engine stopped, repeatedly stall and
crash? Maybe it would not escape the paving and plow
into the weeds or turn sharply and ground-loop or as it
climbed would gradually turn tighter and tighter into a
death spiral or would fly straight as an arrow and disappear beyond the airport into a pear orchard. A little
testing involved grabbing the top of the tail, running,
and a let-go push. It went straight, lifted several inches,
and came back to earth. OK. *Do I dare glide it into the
weeds from above my head with the right amount of push
and the nose pointed slightly down?* I think not. I ran as
fast as I could holding the plane above me, and let go a
few seconds. Seems all right. Go for it.

After several minutes of prop flipping, the engine
roared to life. I pulled out the timer piston shaft which
was adjusted for a thirty second engine run, unclipped
the "booster" battery (keep fingers away from that
prop), grasped the top of the tail, and with a slight push
along the taxi-way the model accelerated and gradually
lifted. The climb steepened, and was going straight.
That would have to be fixed, but looks good; it's not
going to crash. *But what about the glide when the engine
stops? Where will it land?*

ART WEILAND

First Love

Jutting out into Lake Michigan was Navy Pier, my home as a sailor for half a year, following the end of the war. My second Saturday off was time to mix. The guys talked about the Trianon Ballroom on the south side of Chicago and the Aragon Ballroom on the north side. I remembered, when I worked for Douglas Aircraft, the ballroom in Ocean Park next to the pier was the place to be Saturday night. Off to the Trianon on sixty–second street by streetcar, which turned out to be about ninety blocks and two transfers. I entered. Wow, a "big band" was playing forty's music. The entrance area was a dark, red-carpeted lobby, full of scores of standing people, with the ballroom barely visible. About forty girls were standing in one area, and the men were milling around. I'm looking, and getting anxious, then spot the tallest, dark brown hair with bangs girl. I'm moving slowly through the crowd toward her, thinking she'd say I'm with someone, or no thanks, or whatever. With my stomach in a knot, I asked her if she would like to dance, and she accepted. That was a big hurdle for me since it was difficult to ask a girl anything. Also I knew I was a poor dancer.

This seemed all so unnatural for me in a ballroom involved in a pick-up of a lovely, slim, tall lady. Why would she even look at a sailor at the bottom of the Navy totem pole?

We introduced ourselves, Stell and Art. I escorted her into the ballroom that was nothing like I had ever seen: an immense elliptical wood floor bordered with marble columns at least forty feet tall and interrupted by the

270

bandstand, a bar, and the lobby. Above the columns, a balcony, and overhead an elliptical dark blue ceiling with twinkling starlights and glass chandeliers. After a couple dance numbers with no conversation, I'm kind of frozen in time, and no indication she wants to leave me. I asked her if she wanted something to drink. We went up on the balcony with our soft drinks and sat down. That's when I saw what a beautiful lady I had chosen to be with. I began to relax, and the conversation flowed.

After more dancing I asked Stell if I could escort her home. She informed her girl friend, and with Stell picking the streetcars, plus a two-block walk, we were at the bottom of the stairs up to her flat. I asked for her phone number, which she gladly gave. Stell told me the streetcars to take to get back to Navy Pier.

It seemed like a dinner downtown would be a nice first date. The phones on the pier with outside lines were soon going to be a daily walk to talk to Stell. The first call was a dinner invitation. I knocked on her parents' flat (apartment) door. Stell opened the door, and there stood the embodiment of a fashion model on a fashion runway; she was a joy to behold. Some years later she told me it was the first time a guy took her out to dinner. Streetcars were our mode of transportation, which became easy to adapt to as time went on. The ease of conversation with her was a comfortable pleasure. I held her hand on the walk from the streetcar to her flat. Nice. There were cement steps on the stoop and then the bare wooden worn stairs to her front door on the second floor. We kissed goodnight, very nice. After a couple more weekends I was hopelessly in love for the first time, and that love lasted fifty-five years.

Contributors

MICHELLE BARANY (b. 1929) in 1940 moved from Paris, her birthplace, to La Rochelle on France's Atlantic coast, where she grew up.. After completing two baccalaureate degrees, she taught fourth grade for one year and then accepted a position as a translator-interpreter for the general staff of the USAREUR. She and her husband, an American GI, were married in 1955 and moved to the United States in 1956. In the United States, Michelle and Robert, a teacher, lived in Arizona and then California, where they currently make their home. At California State University Long Beach, she completed a double major in English (creative writing option) and French as well as a master's degree in French. They have two daughters, a son, and four grandchildren.

ROBERT BARANY (b. 1931) moved with his family from his birthplace in Republic, Pennsylvania to West Virginia, where he grew up in a coal camp in the Appalachian Mountains. After finishing his bachelor's degree at Fairmont State College in 1953, he taught music in a secondary school and then enlisted in the Army. He was sent to France with an Army band and was stationed, fortuitously, in La Rochelle, the hometown of Michelle, his future wife. Before he was discharged, he and Michelle were married, and he took her from France to

West Virginia. He completed a master's degree at West Virginia University. The couple then spent two years in Arizona, after which they moved to California, where they currently reside.

ROBERT "BUD" BROWER (b. 1928) after graduating from Gilead College (1954) went to Puerto Rico as a missionary for Jehovah's Witnesses. When he returned from his mission (1956), he, in his own words, "did everything." He has been a pattern maker, manufacturer of a unit to conceal garbage cans, and manager of an oil field service company. Currently he writes and dreams.

IRENE CLIFFORD moved to California after forty-five years in New Jersey and Michigan. She has spent her life participating in little theater productions, singing in night clubs and in musical comedies, and, currently, doing volunteer work at regional hospitals.

ROYAL L. CRAIG (b. 1922) spent forty years as an engineer, designing fighter aircraft during World War II and subsequently working on aerospace projects. But his first love, he says, is writing. Currently he is searching for an agent for his just-completed manuscript, *The Ageless Mysticism*. He is hard at work on a new piece, *The Way It Is*, an introduction to the thought process in relation to reality. Among his kudos are The Oregon State Poetry Award and the U.S. Post Office Healthy Aging Award.

GERRY GOODING (b. 1934) grew up in rural Illinois and joined the Air Force in 1952, just a few months after graduating from high school. He spent 26 and one-half years in the Air Force as radio technician instructor, nuclear weapons technician, and satellite ground station manager. When he retired from the Air Force, he entered a new career as test engineer and technical writer. In 1982 he received a bachelor's degree in electronics technology from Chapman University. In 1990 he entered a new career as a freelance Japanese-to-English technical translator. In 1956, he married Aiko Takamine, in Okinawa. In 2005, he retired from translating.

MARY DICKSON JENKINS (b. 1934) lived with her large family in Tyrone, PA, until 1952, when she joined the Navy WAVES. In 1954 she married William Jenkins, a career Navy man, and, with him, had four sons. The couple lived wherever duty called. After the dissolution of the marriage, Mary entered the work force as a grocery checker and also completed an associate of arts degree. Mary says that she is a domestic engineer, specializing in child production and development, and she uses her talents to nurture her four grandchildren.

PAUL SAMMY LARKIN (b. 1932) spent his childhood in Springfield, MO; his home during his teen years was in Amory, MS, but he spent the months of the school year at a parochial boys' school in Arkansas.. In 1950, he entered the Trappist Monastery in Gethsemani, Kentucky, as a lay brother. In 1955, he was one of the Trappist brothers who founded a monastery near Vina, California. In 1963, he left the religious order and ultimately married and came to Southern California, where he became a real estate broker. He and his current wife, Patricia, reside in Huntington Beach, where she works as a speech pathologist.

ANNA PINTER (b. 1939) graduated from Ball State University in 1960, after which she taught art in elementary school in Indiana. She moved to California in 1965. While teaching special education in Whittier and San Gabriel, she completed the work for her California Teaching Credential at California State University Los Angeles. Because of illness, she was forced into early retirement. After her recovery from the long illness, she graduated with honors from the Fashion Institute of Design and Merchandising in Los Angeles. The recurrence of her illness short-circuited her career, and she became a full-time grandmother, allowing her son and two daughters to pursue their own careers. Currently, she reports, she is having fun and enjoying life.

ARTHUR WEILAND (b. 1921) grew up as an Army brat, born in Honolulu and moving every three or four years to the post to which is father was assigned. In 1938, he entered Oregon State College (now University) with a major in mechanical engineering and after two years, entered Curtis Wright Technical Institute in Burbank, California. After graduating from Curtis Wright, he accepted a position with Douglas Aircraft as a draftsman-designer. In 1945, he was drafted and served one year in the United States Navy. Upon his discharge, he returned to Oregon State, and while a student, married Stella Jakimaskus, a union that lasted until her death in 2001. He spent forty-five years as an engineer with Douglas Aircraft (now McDonnell-Douglas), retiring in 1986.

Printed in the United Kingdom
by Lightning Source UK Ltd.
125744UK00001B/14/A